W9-AKE-515

Ex-LIBRIS

The New Order

By the Editors of Time-Life Books

Alexandria, Virginia

The Cover: Buglers and drummers rally the Jungvolk at a Hitler Youth gathering in 1935. Within four years of the Nazi takeover, 90 percent of Germans between the ages of ten and eighteen had joined a youth organization, where they were steeped in propaganda and subjected to strenuous drills as part of the Führer's campaign to foster a militant new Reich.

This volume is one of a series that chronicles the rise and eventual fall of Nazi Germany. Other books in the series include:
The SS
Fists of Steel
Storming to Power

The Third Reich

SERIES DIRECTOR: Thomas H. Flaherty
Series Administrator: Jane Edwin
Editorial Staff for *The New Order:*
Designer: Raymond Ripper
Picture Editor: Jane Jordan
Text Editors: John Newton, Henry Woodhead
Senior Writer: Stephen G. Hyslop
Researchers: Karen Monks, Paula York-Soderlund (principals); Kirk Denkler, Oobie Gleysteen, Jane A. Martin
Assistant Designers: Alan Pitts, Tina Taylor
Copy Coordinator: Charles J. Hagner
Picture Coordinator: Robert H. Wooldridge, Jr.
Editorial Assistant: Patricia D. Whiteford

Special Contributors: Ronald H. Bailey, William S. Heavey, Lydia Preston Hicks, Thomas A. Lewis, Brian C. Pohanka, David R. Thiemann, David S. Thomson (text); Marilyn Murphy (research); Michael Kalen Smith (index)

Editorial Operations
Copy Chief: Diane Ullius
Production: Celia Beattie
Library: Louise D. Forstall

Correspondents: Elisabeth Kraemer-Singh (Bonn); Christine Hinze (London); Christina Lieberman (New York); Maria Vincenza Aloisi (Paris); Ann Natanson (Rome). Valuable assistance was also provided by: Judy Aspinall, Lesley Coleman (London); Elizabeth Brown (New York).

First printing. Printed in U.S.A.

Published simultaneously in Canada.
School and library distribution by Silver Burdett Company, Morristown, New Jersey 07960.

Library of Congress Cataloging in Publication Data
The New order / by the editors of Time-Life Books.
p. cm. — (The Third Reich)
Bibliography: p.
Includes index.
ISBN 0-8094-6962-6.
ISBN 0-8094-6963-4 (lib. bdg.)
1. Germany—Social life and customs—20th century. 2. Germany—Social conditions—1933-1945. 3. National socialism. I. Time-Life Books. II. Series.
DD256.5.N495 1989 943.086—dc19 88-39651

General Consultants

Col. John R. Elting, USA (Ret.), former associate professor at West Point, has written or edited some twenty books, including *Swords around a Throne, The Superstrategists*, and *American Army Life*, as well as *Battles for Scandinavia* in the Time-Life Books World War II series. He was chief consultant to the Time-Life series, The Civil War.

William Sheridan Allen, is chairman of the Department of History at the State University of New York at Buffalo and the author of numerous articles and books on the social and political history of the Weimar Republic and Nazi Germany, including *The Nazi Seizure of Power: The Experience of a Single German Town.* He is also the editor and translator of *The Infancy of Nazism: The Memoirs of Ex-Gauleiter Albert Krebs, 1923-1933,* and has written extensively on the anti-Nazi underground.

Contents

Shoppers in Hanover give patrolling SA men a wide berth in April 1933, shortly after Hitler came to power. "Until the takeover," recalled the man who took this picture, "the Nazis with their brown uniforms did not dare come into our neighborhood."

ONE

The Making of a Nazi Town

Northeim, a picturesque county seat of 10,000 people in 1930, nestled in the gently rolling hills of Germany's Leine River valley. It was a prosperous but unpretentious town, relatively remote from national affairs despite a central location halfway between Bonn and Berlin. Northeim had stood there for a thousand years, and from time to time it had been swept by the winds of history—becoming a hub of commerce in the fifteenth century, a convert to Luther's Reformation a hundred years later, and a last-ditch holdout against Catholic arms in the seventeenth century's Thirty Years' War. Yet for most of its millennium, Northeim had lived quietly, at peace with itself and with its neighbors.

Across Germany were towns of modest size and aspirations much like Northeim. They were ordinary places, populated by people doing everyday things as the fourth decade of the twentieth century began. But Germany was about to change almost beyond recognition. These same people would soon become accomplices to the malignity of Adolf Hitler's Reich.

Hitler's rise to power was not the result of any public affirmation of his dark concept of racial purity and world domination; it was much more the product of national despair, confusion, and fear. His use of power would be characterized not by the efficient domination of every aspect of German society, as he intended, but by incompetence, corruption, and violence. The party he forged as a weapon with which to seize power proved ill equipped to administer the affairs of the country. In order to function, his new state would have to rely on many of the people and institutions that he had intended to destroy.

The National Socialist conquest of Germany would depend on the emotions and thoughts, the needs and dreams of common folk such as the burghers of Northeim. How Hitler reached out to them and how they responded were key elements in his ascendancy to the dictatorship. As one German said of his neighbors, "They slowly stumbled from their lower-middle-class dream into an era of greatness. Now they felt wonderful, were enormously proud of what the man had made of them. They never un-

In a sylvan setting outside the town of Northeim in central Germany, world-war veterans in wheelchairs are honored in 1938 by the War Victims' Association. In Northeim as elsewhere, the Nazis had absorbed local organizations such as veterans' groups to ensure their adherence to the new order.

The Nazi party in Germany in 1936 was organized in thirty-one gaus, or districts, that were run by party officials called gauleiters. Many of the local leaders had no experience in government and proved woefully inept.

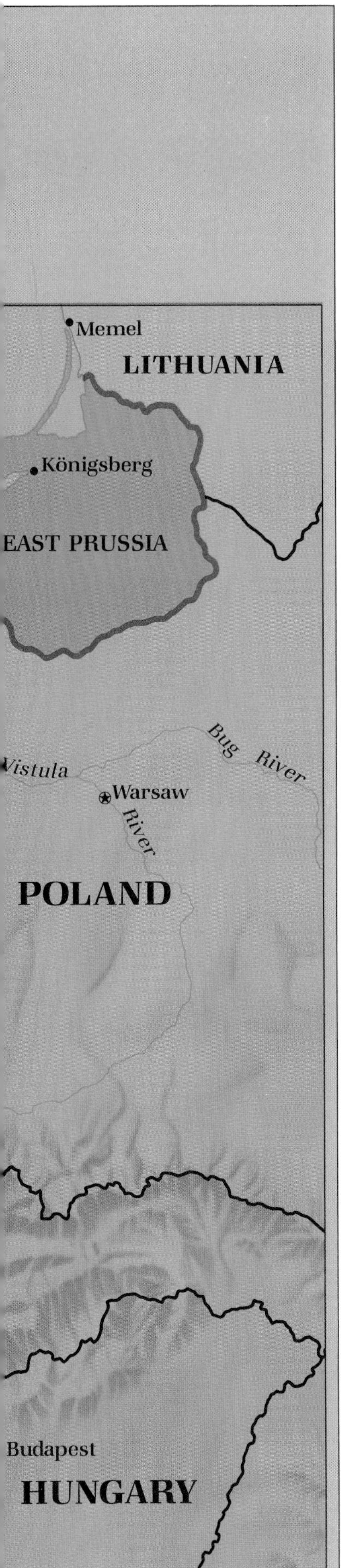

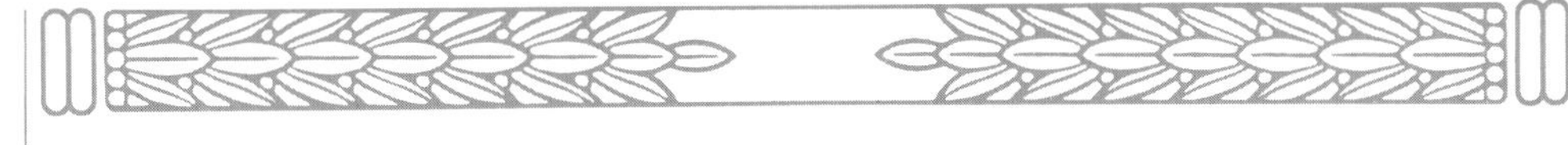

derstood that it was they—all of them together—who first made the man."

It took a succession of momentous and unsettling changes—rapid industrialization, a lost war, a failed revolution, and finally a smothering depression—to create in Northeim and in Germany an atmosphere in which nazism could thrive. Industrialization came late to Germany, and its arrival was disruptive. Modern production methods had been common in Britain and France for nearly a hundred years before they appeared in Germany, following the unification of the country under Prince Otto von Bismarck in 1871. Then change accelerated, and German life was wrenched to the core as people abandoned their family farms and village shops to seek a better life as wage earners in the larger population centers.

Late in the nineteenth century, the new era reached Northeim on the wheels of two new railroad lines that intersected there. The sleepy tempo of the market town soon picked up, and in the half-century that followed, Northeim's population more than doubled. The townspeople had evolved a rigid caste system of attitude and place that affected their lives in many ways. The old families, who could trace their roots back for generations, lived in the oldest section of town. Surrounded by a medieval wall, their half-timbered houses with steep slate roofs were crowded together along the narrow cobblestone streets that radiated from a central square. Once their neighborhood had formed virtually the entire town, but by 1930, relative newcomers who lived outside the walled section composed three-fourths of the population.

West of the old town, toward the Leine River, sprawled an area of lower-class housing where most of the townspeople lived, close to the few industries and the large railroad yards that employed them. To the north, between the walled section and the banks of the Ruhme River, near its confluence with the Leine, lived the middle class, mostly civil servants working for the railroad and for agencies of the provincial and state governments. The small minority of well-to-do Northeimers clustered in elevated splendor on a hill rising south of the old town. The distinctions were much more than geographic. The native families resented the newcomers. The hillside residents, along with many of the sedate civil servants, looked down with suspicion and fear on the Marxists proselytizing among the working-class tenements. The town's 9,000 Protestants were uncomfortable with its 600 Catholics and 120 Jews.

The world war had added new and bitter divisions to those already existing in Northeim and in Germany as a whole. An entire generation of young men had been yanked from home and community, traumatized by war, and so confused by the surrender of their armies and the dismantling of their government that few knew how to face the future. For many

veterans, the only remaining option was to hate—hate the enemies who had defeated them, the "traitors" who had capitulated, the communists who threatened revolution, and eventually even the Weimar government that offered no answers.

Many who wanted to work learned that whole categories of jobs had vanished because of technological changes that occurred with increasing rapidity in the 1920s. New mass-production methods were making the work of individual artisans unprofitable. One result of this was that even though 25 million Germans were classified as laborers in 1925, as many as 45 million—three-fourths of the population—were earning laborer's wages without hope of advancement. Those who had managed to reach the ranks of white-collar workers found themselves trapped in a similar way. Although they possessed a degree of professional qualification and skill, they discovered that the traditional passports to success were no longer valid. Disarmament, the payment of reparations, and economic upheaval in the aftermath of war had eliminated opportunities for promotion to high positions in the military and civil service. As one journalist observed, "The way to the top is blocked off."

Unable to advance, many among the middle class sought to improve their prospects during the 1920s by opening retail shops. Always a respectable occupation, shopkeeping held the traditional promise of independence and security. Between 1907 and 1925, the number of retail outlets in Germany increased by 21 percent. But shopkeepers, too, found their prospects reduced and their livelihood threatened by new forms of retailing, such as department stores and mail-order catalogs. Small farms, long a bastion of independent well-being, did not escape the national malaise. Mechanization had not reached the German farm; in one typical district, half the farms were smaller than 12.5 acres, and three-fourths of them had no machinery of any kind. For years, these inefficient little operations had been propped up by the protectionist policies of the kaiser, the insatiable demands of the wartime economy, and the postwar inflation that eroded the value of currency while increasing the relative value of food. With the disappearance of these conditions after 1924, the farmers—who composed 30 percent of the population—suddenly found themselves on the brink of disaster.

The Weimar government, accused by extremist groups of bringing on all these disastrous changes, devoted its fiercest efforts to maintaining the status quo and thus made conditions worse. The government might have eased the stresses of industrialization by assisting the process—for example, by helping to develop the water-power resources of eastern Germany. Instead, it concentrated on stifling change, in one case by passing

Fascinated villagers in rural Hesse assemble around a truck equipped with loudspeakers to hear the left-of-center message of the Social Democrats in the 1930 election campaign. The Social Democratic party, number one on the ballot, was defending its position as Germany's largest political organization.

homestead legislation to entice former servicemen into the sector of the economy that needed them least—farming.

Government ineptitude not only engendered a widespread loss of confidence but promoted a new national sentiment, the *völkisch* movement. Shortly after the end of the war, fully seventy-five unions, societies, and federations proclaimed the *völkisch* doctrine, although no one could say exactly what the doctrine was. It involved belief in the inherent superiority of the German race, nation, and culture. Adherents expressed their pride

by partaking of a mystical communion of German nationalism that was available only to those of pure Aryan race. And they devoutly believed that this racial superiority could be contaminated not only by crossbreeding with allegedly inferior races, such as the Jews, Slavs, and Poles, but by mere social contact with them.

Prejudice against Jews was not new in Germany. As early as the Middle Ages, Jews had been restricted to specified occupations and required to live in segregated neighborhoods. They had frequently been made scapegoats during times of social upheaval, but seldom so vindictively as under the Weimar Republic. During this period, they became highly visible; just as unemployment worsened, Jews fleeing persecution in Russia and Poland streamed into the country and competed with the native Germans for scarce jobs. Meanwhile, *völkisch* orators denounced Jews as outsiders, defilers of the Nordic race—and worse. Fabricated stories abounded, relating grisly details of Jewish ritual murders of Christians and of Jewish plots to seize worldwide political power. The Jews represented less than one percent of the German population—too little to pose an actual threat to the well-being of non-Jewish natives. Nevertheless, the imagined peril grew larger in the fearful minds of the *völkisch* faithful.

A Nazi campaign poster urges workers to support Hitler, the "front-line soldier." The Nazis tried with little success to entice blue-collar voters away from their traditional parties, the Communists and Socialists.

The political, economic, and racial fissures in German society grew deeper and wider through the 1920s. Every point of view was represented by a political party, from the Communists and Social Democrats on the left, through the moderate Catholic Centrists, to the monarchist Nationalists on the right. So many parties were spread across the spectrum of political belief that forming a coalition large and stable enough to support everyday government became increasingly difficult. Of all the political organizations, only the fringe groups of the far right, including the National Socialist German Workers' party, or Nazi party, appealed to the conservative middle class—the people who longed not only for solutions to the problems besieging Germany but for a return to the order that had once characterized German life.

During the late 1920s, the party of Adolf Hitler was hardly a major force anywhere in Germany, including the town of Northeim. The first of a sprinkling of Nazis in Northeim was a bookstore owner named Wilhelm Spannaus. He had worked as a teacher in South America from 1912 to 1921 and was appalled by the conditions he found on his return. "I had left Germany at the height of the power and glory of the Wilhelmine Reich," he said later. "I came back to find the fatherland

Impoverished citizens of Deesbach, a village in Thuringia, wait as the mayor signs permits allowing them to beg in the streets. Throughout Germany, the depression turned workers into beggars, a plight the Nazis vigorously hastened to exploit.

in shambles, under a socialist republic." He settled on the Nazis as the only group dedicated to the restoration of German greatness.

A kind, intelligent man from an old Northeim family, Spannaus was well liked and highly respected, chairman of the town's lecture society and a leader of its Lutheran church. "Wilhelm Spannaus bears a heavy burden," a town resident recalled years later, with more regret than anger, "for it was mainly his example that led many people to join the Nazis."

Another early Nazi in Northeim provided a vivid contrast to Spannaus. He was Ernst Girmann, who had returned from the war with a wound, an Iron Cross, and a rage that consumed him. He had worked in his father's hardware store before the war but afterward showed no interest in business or any other career. He drank heavily, reviled his fellow townspeople, burst into frequent, violent rages, and after 1922 advanced the National Socialist cause with brutal fanaticism. On one occasion, he was sentenced to two months in jail for caning a member of a socialist paramilitary group, shouting, "I'll beat you to death!" According to a Northeim civil servant, there were two kinds of Nazis in the town: "the decent ones and the gutter type. In the end, the gutter won out."

At first, however, few people paid attention to either type of Nazi. Despite serious economic problems, times were relatively good in Germany and seemed to be improving. It was not yet apparent that this was a false

prosperity, based on large loans from abroad that would one day come due with disastrous consequences. But while there was hope, the Nazis could make no headway. In 1925, the party had only a dozen members in Northeim, and by 1928 the roll had shrunk to five. The reduction might have continued if the New York stock-market crash of 1929 had not caused the Great Depression's ponderous ripples to spread around the world.

In Northeim, the onset of the depression was marked only by a slight rise in unemployment that affected a few factory workers. Because so many of the working residents were civil servants employed by the railroad or government agencies, there was no large-scale loss of jobs and no consequent failure of businesses and banks. Yet the first, mild signs of distress set off a disproportionate wave of fear among the people least affected—the artisans, shopkeepers, farmers, and white-collar workers of the middle class. As late as the autumn of 1931, they were able to count only 418 townspeople among the unemployed, but they watched in mounting apprehension as more than 9,000 jobless workers trudged into town from the surrounding area to collect unemployment benefits and, when those ran out, welfare payments. They saw the depression consuming the world and saw their government impotent in the face of it.

People in distress were particularly vulnerable to Hitler's blandishments. He had a genius for using the pent-up frustration and anger of the disaffected as an energy source to fuel his quest for personal power. First, however, Hitler had to attract the people's attention. He had spent the lean years organizing on a massive scale, dividing his party's political organization into districts, called gaus, that corresponded roughly to the country's electoral districts. Their chairmen, the gauleiters, were responsible for transmitting the party line, in the form of propaganda and directives, to local groups such as the one in Northeim.

The Nazi party depended for its income on membership dues and the sale of tickets to its events. Speakers who did not fill their halls, events that did not pay their way, and recruiting methods that did not attract enough new members were discarded. The successful appeals—those directed to farmers, shopkeepers, and small-business owners—were retained and polished. Thus the party gained valuable experience at the same time it laid the groundwork for expansion.

In Northeim as elsewhere, the harangues of Nazis such as Ernst Girmann began to make sense once the depression struck. In the spring of 1929, the handful of party members in town had begun to hold weekly public meetings in a room provided by the sympathetic owner of the cattle-auction hall. In these rustic surroundings, Nazi speakers discussed topics with such tested titles as "Breaking the Serfdom of Interest Payments" or

The Limbo of the Unemployed

When his son Herbert was born in 1930, Karl Döhler had not held a full-time job for five years. As one of four million unemployed German workers, Döhler had plenty of time for his child—hours devoted to exploring the narrow streets and outlying fields of his native Hanover. "He built a little seat for me on his bicycle," recalled Herbert years later, "and every day, off we would go."

The elder Döhler seemed condemned to spend his most productive years in a limbo of enforced idleness and grinding poverty. A locksmith by trade, he supplemented the family's meager monthly welfare payment by repairing bicycles and taking occasional odd jobs. Otherwise, he simply killed time—as is poignantly recorded on these pages in photographs first published in a 1932 magazine. Titled "One of Millions," the story documented the quiet despair of Germany's jobless underclass.

Eventually, the ascendant Nazi party and rearmament created jobs that saved workers from spirit-breaking unemployment. Döhler concealed his long-held socialist convictions and went to work in a local aircraft factory—silently taking his place in the new order.

Karl Döhler gazes through a shop window at clothes he cannot afford. A new suit cost more than his family's monthly budget of sixty-four marks.

Two-year-old Herbert eats in his own chair while his parents dine at the kitchen table. Typically, the Döhlers' main meal was a stew of beans, barley, or turnips, purchased at the local soup kitchen for fifteen pfennigs.

Döhler assembles a bicycle outside his home. A natural handyman, he pieced together old parts and sold the rebuilt bikes to add to his income.

Döhler and his friends play cards outside the Workers' Sports Club, a popular hangout for Hanover's unemployed.

A picture of lonely introspection, Döhler—out of work for seven years by 1932—succumbs to melancholy in his kitchen.

Karl Döhler tenderly holds his son's arm on a walk through the *Altstadt,* the oldest part of Hanover.

"The Protocols of the Wise Men of Zion." The first meeting attracted only 15 people. By the end of the year, however, the Nazis could boast a vigorous group of 58 members from Northeim and vicinity, and a meeting on the subject of the Marxist betrayal of the German workers drew 120 people.

It was not easy for a Northeim citizen to determine what the Nazis stood for; in general, their goal seemed to be the creation of a rejuvenated *völkisch* community enjoying military strength and national pride. But it was not difficult to see what the Nazis were against. Girmann and his little band resented the present state of affairs in Germany and were sure who was to blame for it. Their villains were the Weimar government, with its liberal, democratic ways; the Marxists, who had stirred up the workers and disrupted the country; and the Jews, who had somehow profited from Germany's misery. And if some of the message was muddled, the messengers undeniably had spirit and conviction.

The vagueness of the Nazi program enabled it to be all things to all people. In contrast, rival parties made specific appeals to narrow ideological or economic factions. To woo factory workers, the Nazis sang socialist songs (with modified lyrics), called one another by the Marxist honorific *comrade,* and waved red flags. When speaking to farmers, party orators beatified the peasant and promised a more traditional society in which those who toiled on the land would be afforded the respect they deserved. Middle-class audiences delighted in Nazi denunciations of the rich capitalists who oppressed them, the left-wing workers who threatened them, and the democratic government that did nothing to help them.

Ever attentive to ticket sales, the Northeim Nazis and their gauleiter selected from their repertoire those themes that worked best in the town. Northeimers did not respond well to rabid anti-Semitism, so the Nazi speakers were instructed to tone down that theme. The overwhelmingly Lutheran town was, however, interested in religious matters, so the Nazis emphasized something called "positive Christianity"—and drew solid support from Lutheran pastors.

Those who looked beyond the emotional appeals for a specific program were referred to the party manifesto, the Twenty-five Points. This list of positions and demands included expressions of virulent racism, inflammatory nationalism, and unqualified contempt for the policies and institutions of the Weimar government. Presented as the inviolable tenets of nazism, the points in fact included something for everyone, frequently contradicted one another, and were ambiguous enough to support any action the party felt inclined to take. The intellectual poverty of the party philosophy was demonstrated unintentionally by one Nazi speaker who shouted to a group of farmers: "We don't want higher bread prices! We

don't want lower bread prices! We don't want unchanged bread prices! We want National Socialist bread prices!"

Such fervent nonsense impressed few people. But many among the middle class admired the Nazis' muscular opposition to the Social Democrats—the so-called Marxists who dominated the Weimar government and were thus held responsible for everything that had gone wrong since the war. And the Nazi themes of patriotism and militarism drew highly emotional responses from people who could not forget Germany's prewar imperial grandeur. Most important of all, the Nazis seemed to be promising an end to the depression. As a reporter for a Northeim newspaper recalled: "Most of those who joined the Nazis did so because they wanted a radical answer to the economic problem. Then, too, people wanted a hard, sharp, clear leadership—they were disgusted with the eternal political strife of parliamentary party politics."

Helmeted municipal police search amused Storm Troopers for concealed weapons before allowing them into town in 1932. When Hitler became chancellor, he lifted such restrictions and unleashed the armed SA against foes of the Nazi party.

In the national elections of September 1930, the Nazis garnered nearly 6.5 million votes and became second only to the Social Democrats as the most popular party in Germany. In Northeim, where in 1928 Nazi candidates had received 123 votes, they now polled 1,742, a respectable 28 percent of the total. The nationwide success engendered even faster growth; in just three years, party membership would rise from about 100,000 to almost a million, and the number of local branches would increase tenfold. The new members included working-class people (nearly half of them unemployed), farmers, and middle-class professionals. They were both better educated and younger—fully 70 percent of them were not yet forty years old—than the Old Fighters, who had been the backbone of the party during its first decade. The Nazis now presented themselves as the party of the young, the strong, and the pure, in opposition to an establishment populated by the elderly, the weak, and the dissolute.

In Northeim, 191 people had joined the local Nazi group by May of 1931. Although only one-third of the members were townspeople and the rest were from the surrounding county, the group was now strong enough to influence town affairs. That summer, the national banks began to totter, and the central government had to declare a bank holiday. There was no general panic in Northeim, but a local cooperative bank failed and later a branch bank closed. Members of the town's conservative middle class became ever more anxious.

As the Weimar government approached paralysis in 1932, it called election after election in an increasingly desperate effort to create a majority coalition in the Reichstag that could perform the basic tasks of government. In Northeim as elsewhere in Germany, these elections were marked by feverish Nazi politicking and violence aimed at intimidating the opposition. Uniformed members of the party's police force, the Sturmabteilung, or SA, were brutal. Northeim had only about fifty of these Storm Troopers at the time, but for parades or planned riots they were joined by reinforcements from outlying areas, giving the impression that hundreds of Nazi street fighters were loose in Northeim. "There was a feeling of restless energy about the Nazis," a Northeim woman recalled. "You constantly saw the sidewalks painted with swastikas or littered by pamphlets put out by the Nazis. I was drawn by the feeling of strength about the party, even though there was much in it that was highly questionable."

It was in towns such as Northeim that the Nazis acquired their mass constituency. While they never gained a majority in the country as a whole, the party became essential to the formation of any workable coalition that could end the governmental crisis. By 1933, German conservatives dominating the national cabinet determined to buy Hitler cheaply and harness the National Socialists to their own cause. In January, President Hindenburg reluctantly appointed Hitler chancellor of Germany and asked him to form a coalition government. Instead, Hitler dissolved the Reichstag and called yet another national election, convinced that with the advantages of the chancellorship and the growing strength of his party, he could remove all effective opposition.

The campaign tactics employed in Northeim were typical. Under orders from Hermann Göring, who acted in his capacity as Prussian minister of the interior, the town police prohibited public demonstrations by Communists on the pretext of preventing violence. The police searched the residences of Communist party members for what one newspaper described as "forbidden literature," and they confiscated the most recent issue of the Social Democrats' newspaper because it contained an article that ridiculed Hitler. In February, when the Social Democrats tried to stage

Guarded by Storm Troopers, political opponents of the regime are forced to scrub anti-Hitler slogans from the side of a building shortly after the Nazis had come to power in 1933.

a rally in Northeim's market square, the police herded them into a nearby beer hall and surrounded it while National Socialists strutted in the streets outside. It was the last time Northeim's Social Democrats would attempt to hold a meeting during the life of the Third Reich. The message was clear: The Nazis intended to brook no opposition. The Social Democrats felt utterly defeated. That night, one of them, a former railroad worker named Hermann Schulze, carefully folded his party flag, placed it in a coffee can, and buried it in a field.

On the night of February 27, an arsonist burned the Reichstag building in Berlin, and Hitler insisted that the communists had done it to signal a new workers' revolution. The next day, he persuaded President Hindenburg to issue an emergency decree suspending all civil liberties. Freed of legal restraints, Hitler unleashed the Storm Troopers to arrest opponents, shut down their publications, confiscate their campaign materials, and break up their meetings. In the March elections, the Nazis, together with their Nationalist party allies, won 52 percent of the votes cast and forged a dominant coalition in the Reichstag. Less than three weeks later, Hitler bludgeoned the legislature into passing an Enabling Act that transferred to his cabinet the power to approve pieces of legislation, set the budget, make foreign treaties, and amend the constitution. Democratic government in Germany was finished.

Hitler's first priority was to make Germany safe for his dictatorship. He wanted nothing less than the complete nazification of the country and all

VOLKSWILLE
VOLKSWILLE
VOLKSWILLE

At left, a crowd in Hanover watches an agile Nazi hoist a swastika over the Union Building at midday on April 1, 1933. Minutes earlier, an SS squad had stormed the building and torn down the flag of the Social Democratic party, setting it afire on the sidewalk outside. At right, SA men watch an opposition flag burn on the terrace of the city hall in Magdeburg.

its institutions; he called it *Gleichschaltung*, a euphemism roughly meaning coordination. He first used the term when he ordered the states to bring the representation in their legislatures into line with the composition of the Reichstag, done so the Nazis could dominate everywhere by an equal margin. But it soon was evident that the concept was much broader than that. Hitler intended to make his party not merely the leading party in Germany, but the only one—to impose his will not just on the policymaking of government, but on every level of its operations, from the national parliament to the local police station. Nor was it enough that his party and his government obey him with unquestioning loyalty; he wanted the same response from German organizations of every kind.

Hitler would not achieve total domination overnight. The public's initial response to his seizure of power was an unseemly rush to share in the fruits of victory and help shape the future. By the end of April 1933, the Nazi party had grown by 150 percent to 1.5 million members. But newfound victory was just as stressful for the Nazis as past defeat. The party had always been racked by differences over how the new Germany should be run. Since plans had been vague, however, it had been possible to smooth over disagreements by concentrating on the first priority—winning control of the government. After control had been won, however, theoretical differences became serious conflicts.

The gauleiters, for example, assumed they would run the victorious party—and hence the new state. Instead, they found themselves competing with newer party members, who in some districts outnumbered the Old Fighters by four to one. For their part, the Storm Troopers had always disdained politics and politicians and believed SA men would hold the real power by taking over the regular army, which they were now eager to do. Meanwhile, another element of the party, Heinrich Himmler's black-shirted Schutzstaffel, or SS, wanted to become the nation's police force, the better to control the activities of the populace. Soon, in addition to the existing party units, any number of affiliated organizations sprouted. Nazi doctors, lawyers, civil servants, and others built their own bureaucracies and joined the struggle for power.

Each organization thought it was fulfilling Hitler's intentions and looked to him for support. Each was puzzled when he failed to respond as its members wished. They did not suspect that he never intended them to assume a significant share of the power. Hitler was determined that no individual or group should have the chance to challenge his leadership, and one of his preventive methods was to keep them enmeshed in a murky, overlapping structure that few could understand, let alone dominate. Affairs became hopelessly tangled, with no one sure who outranked whom. As late as 1943, a gauleiter defied even the head of the SS. "Himmler cannot tell me anything," he said. "If something is to be ordered, Hitler will have to do it, and it will be followed." That is what Hitler intended all along: that no one could act without somehow invoking the will of the Führer. Yet for all his accumulated and jealously guarded power, he displayed a remarkable aversion to giving direct orders or making choices.

"Hitler hesitates to make a decision no matter how small," wrote one of his close associates. The Führer found it nearly impossible to fire anyone; it was much easier to give another person duplicate authority for the same job. In affairs of state, as in party matters, Hitler preferred to let his subordinates squabble. Ministers were instructed to present papers for his signature only after all disagreements had been ironed out. Hitler called meetings only when they were unavoidable, and when he did so, no one was allowed to raise a difference of opinion unless it had been specifically authorized. Yet these same ministers were forbidden to meet when Hitler was not present—even informally, over a stein of beer. It was feared that they might form a cabal against him.

Hitler's aversion to meetings made his large, informal daily lunches prime opportunities for underlings to gain backing for personal projects. At table, party leaders attempted to steer the conversation in the desired direction, aware that a word from Hitler could be interpreted as a com-

mand. The gambit was risky, however; an offhand comment could hurt a career if it contradicted Hitler's set opinions.

The inevitable result of this lack of direction was waste and inefficiency throughout the structures of the party and the state. In the words of one disgusted gauleiter, "Almost every leadership task is dealt with in at least two party offices, sometimes three." Likewise, in government matters Hitler often ignored the existing machinery; he created special authorities under favored individuals in order to accomplish particular assignments. Without consulting the Reich Ministry of Transport, for example, the Führer gave Fritz Todt, a colonel on Himmler's staff as well as a civil engineer, the responsibility for "overall supervision of German roads, with the objective of building a large-scale network of autobahns." Todt assumed many of the powers of the transport minister, exercised substantial legislative authority, and dominated the construction industry. What came to be known as Organization Todt was soon functioning as a formidable fiefdom within the state.

Those closer than Todt to Hitler received much broader grants of power. Hermann Göring accumulated an impressive list of titles—Prussian minister president and minister of the interior, Reich commissioner for aviation, Reich forestry commissioner, and controller of the hunt. But the titles did not even begin to define the range of his power. He not only commanded the Luftwaffe but conducted foreign negotiations for the Führer without the knowledge of the Foreign Ministry. Göring's research bureau in the Aviation Ministry tapped the telephones of government officials and eavesdropped on foreign diplomatic communications. The bureau employed hundreds of technicians—none of whom had anything at all to do with aviation research.

In 1933, Hitler appointed Rudolf Hess, who had served in prison with him and taken dictation for Hitler's book *Mein Kampf,* to the post of deputy führer. Hess, along with his shrewd and ambitious assistant, Martin Bormann, thought he had a mandate to create a supreme party command that would dominate all aspects of society. But Hitler at once undercut Hess's authority by elevating Robert Ley, who would successfully nazify Germany's labor unions, to a parallel position as the party's organizational leader. The two men feuded bitterly throughout the 1930s as each sought to gain the upper hand. While thus engaged, they posed no threat to Hitler, and he never intervened to resolve the conflict.

Amid all this confusion, someone had to process the everyday, humdrum details of government. By default, those tasks remained the responsibility of the civil servants who had always performed them. Most prominent among these bureaucrats was Hans Lammers, head of the Reich

Chancellery. A bald, colorless man, Lammers accumulated great power by controlling the enormous flow of state papers requiring action—a job for which few Nazis had the temperament. Lammers and his staff of a dozen civil servants handled about 600 communications each day, seeing to it that the forms were properly filled out and that the niceties of bureaucratic etiquette were observed.

Far from encouraging such efficiency and attention to detail, Hitler was contemptuous of it. "The civil service is the refuge of mediocre talents," he proclaimed, adding that a bureaucrat "must be regarded as a man deficient by nature, or else deformed by usage." His attitude, combined with his haphazard style of governing, only created friction between pugnacious party stalwarts and the professional bureaucrats who had heretofore enjoyed considerable status. The civil service had occupied a prominent place in German government and society for two centuries, since the time of Frederick the Great. Applicants for the higher-ranking jobs had to possess a doctorate and pass rigorous examinations. If successful, they were appointed for life. Thus most civil servants enjoyed financial security, looked down on the push and shove of politics, and were conservative and nationalistic. As a group, they were receptive to the Nazi doctrine of state supremacy, but they failed to share in the National Socialists' fanaticism and zealotry. Most of the party, including a majority of the Old Fighters, suspected civil servants of being an elitist group that showed little commitment to the ideals of a *völkisch* community. Nazi leaders feared the power of the bureaucrats and argued for their replacement, at least at the top, by reliable members of the party.

This notion proved hard to accomplish, however. There were simply not enough qualified Nazis to run all the government ministries and bureaus. A great many party functionaries were quick to grasp local offices: 4,000 group leaders and 60 percent of the district leaders took over as mayors of their towns and cities. But these party hacks lacked the education and experience needed for managing an industrial state. Most could barely cope with the rudiments of their new jobs. As a result, few Nazi bureaucrats advanced to the middle or upper levels of the government. After five years of Nazi rule, only five of the thirty-eight departments in the Reich ministries were run by party members—and all five of those individuals had joined after 1933. Moreover, once they undertook government responsibilities, party members gave their allegiance to the state first and the party second. As early as 1933, Hermann Göring refused to consult the party when appointing government officials.

When a professional civil servant was replaced by a Nazi, efficiency and morale usually plummeted. This happened when Freiherr Eltz von Rue-

A Profusion of Gleaming Blades

On December 15, 1933, the SA authorized its members to carry a new side arm—a Renaissance-style dagger. Other Nazi organizations were quick to follow, and before long branches of the uniform-conscious civil service were also clamoring for daggers of their own. Hitler, keenly interested in his followers' regalia and eager to support the world-renowned German blade makers' cartel in Solingen, approved many of the designs himself.

Most new designs were created by students and masters at the state trade schools. Once a pattern had been selected, it was submitted to the Reich Goods Center for final approval. Only then could organization members purchase and display their new side arms.

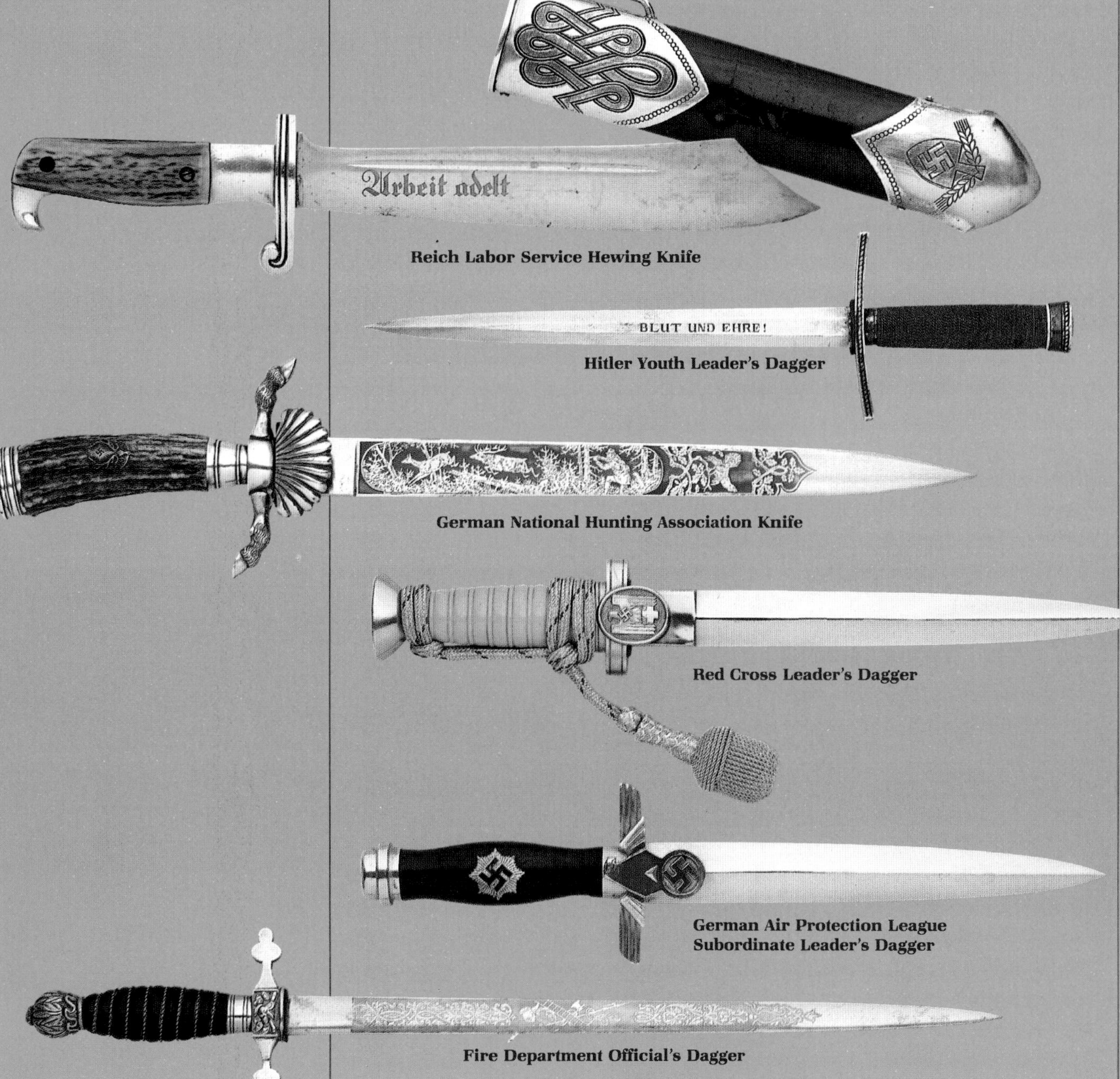

Reich Labor Service Hewing Knife

Hitler Youth Leader's Dagger

German National Hunting Association Knife

Red Cross Leader's Dagger

German Air Protection League Subordinate Leader's Dagger

Fire Department Official's Dagger

benach, a Catholic conservative in charge of the Postal and Transportation Ministries, was dismissed from both of his posts. A holdover from the 1933 coalition cabinet, Eltz had seen to it that the bureaus in his charge continued to function efficiently. In a generous mood, Hitler offered him the Nazis' highest honor, the golden party badge. Believing that one had to be a party member in order to receive the badge, Eltz hesitated to accept it, and an infuriated Hitler forced him to resign. Two stalwart National Socialists took over the ministries—and immediately began to feud. While their organizations disintegrated, the Nazis found they could agree on only two things: their anti-Semitism and their opposition to any party interference in their ministries.

As the source of legal justification for everything done during the Third Reich, the Ministry of the Interior became the chief battleground for the struggle between the National Socialists and the civil servants. Hitler's

Working as a team in 1933, a Brownshirt *(left)* and an SS man cover a display window with a poster that urges German citizens not to buy from Jews.

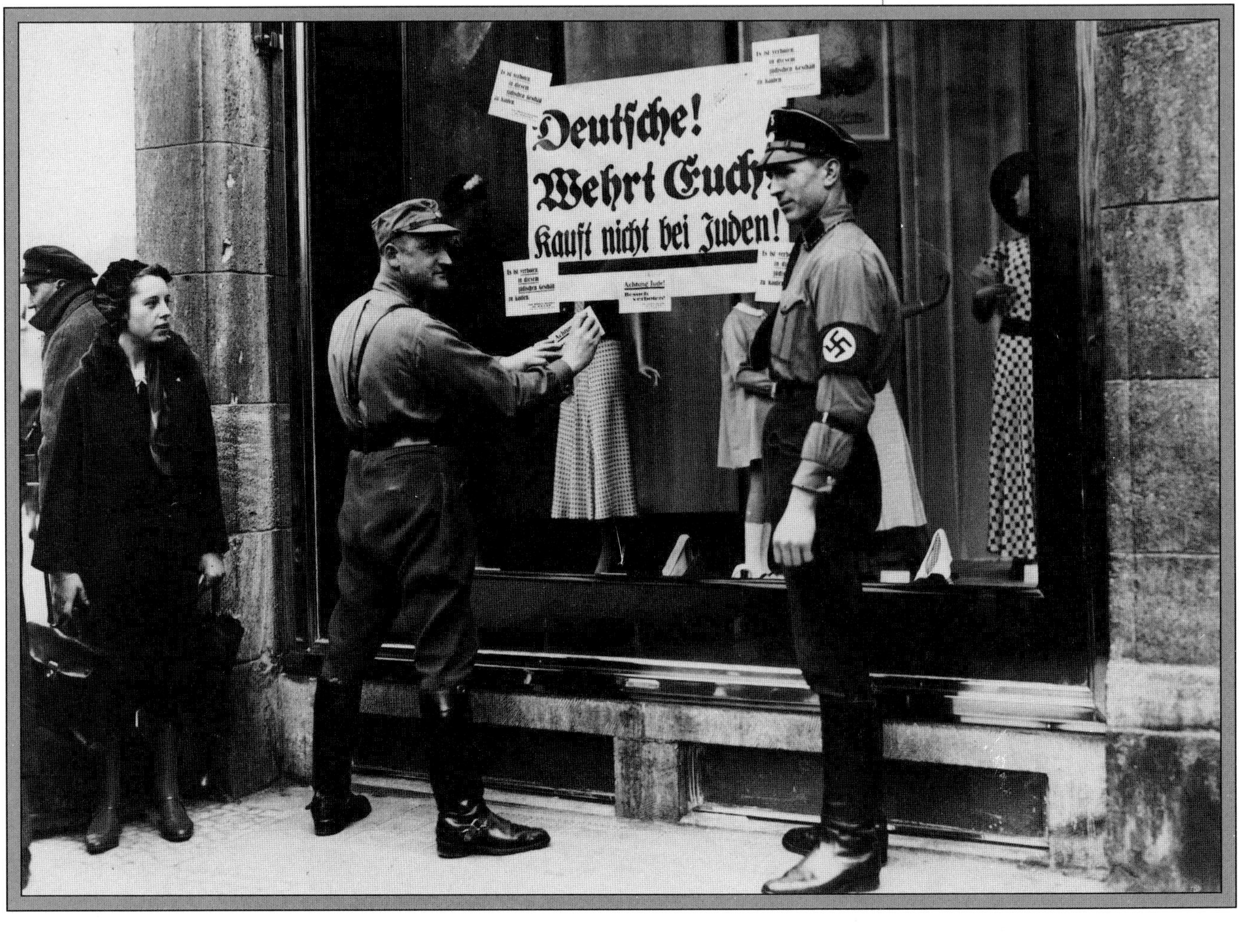

A Jewish man and a non-Jewish woman in Hamburg are forced to wear placards revealing their alleged cohabitation—a breach of the anti-Semitic Nuremberg Laws of 1935. The woman's inscription proclaims, "I am the greatest swine, who can have relations only with Jews." The man's reads, "As a Jew, I always get the most beautiful German girls into my bedroom."

interior minister was Wilhelm Frick, a former Munich police official who had befriended Hitler before the 1923 Beer Hall Putsch. A quiet man, more at ease among his stacks of paper than with the rowdy crowd surrounding the Führer, Frick soon emerged as a champion of civil servants resisting the encroachment of the party.

In April 1933, Frick's ministry introduced the Law for the Re-creation of the Professional Civil Service. This was Frick's attempt to limit and regulate the purging of the government. While the new law provided for the firing of Jews, Communists, and Social Democrats, it did not require that a civil servant be dismissed for failure to join the Nazi party. As a result, a wholesale purge of the country's 1.5 million civil servants was averted, and only about five percent lost their jobs on racial or political grounds (although the ever-present threat of removal made the remaining civil servants a besieged and demoralized group).

Even such limited triumphs of legalism were rare in Hitler's Germany. A more typical example of the chaotic process and baleful results of lawmaking in the Third Reich was the advent of the Nuremberg Laws of 1935. Ever since Hitler came to power, hard-line racists in the party had argued for increased repression of the Jews, especially boycotts of Jewish-owned businesses. While Hitler had resisted boycotts because he feared they would hurt the economy, lower-ranking National Socialist minions all across the country organized random assaults on Jewish-owned shops. It became obvious that Hitler had to enunciate a policy on the issue or risk losing control of his party.

On the night before his appearance at the annual party rally at Nuremberg in 1935, Hitler decided that his prepared address lacked teeth. He summoned Frick, whose Interior Ministry dealt with citizenship issues and therefore with the question of the status of Jews. At midnight, Hitler ordered Frick to draft a new law cracking down on the Jews. As Frick understood it, the Führer required "some pithy statement giving preference to those with German blood."

Hitler, however, expected much more than that, and he rejected several drafts written during the night until he got what he wanted. At the rally the next morning, Hitler issued two proclamations that for the first time draped his rabid anti-Semitism with the legal trappings of state policy. The first denied Jews the right of citizenship, which was reserved for people of "German or kindred blood." The second, titled the Law for the Protection of German Blood and German Honor, forbade marriage or extramarital sexual relations between Jews and German citizens. German honor was further secured by prohibiting Jews from employing as domestic help any German woman aged forty-five or younger, and by denying Jews the right to display the national colors. These epochal laws—which served notice that the Jewish nightmare had officially begun—had been slapped together overnight on the Führer's whim.

As it was in other areas of government, Hitler's participation in the legal system continued to be haphazard. He apparently had no desire to change the body of civil law affecting such things as wills and commercial contracts. Criminal law was another matter. Backed by the necessary statutes, he could deprive his opponents not only of their power to resist him, but of their freedom and even of their lives. In addition to legislation, he would of course need the compliance of judges and lawyers.

Like the civil service, the judiciary was a close-knit, educated elite sharing conservative, authoritarian views not far removed from Nazi doctrine. But despite their status as members of a learned profession and their lack of hostility to nazism, attorneys and judges were not spared Hitler's paranoid hand. All German lawyers were required to join the Nazi Lawyers' Association and submit to its peculiar discipline. So-called honor courts reprimanded members who neglected to render the Hitler salute and disbarred those who failed to vote in a Reichstag election or national plebiscite. Court procedure, buffeted by the legal innovations of the new

Wearing new swastika-and-eagle badges on their robes, judges of Berlin's criminal courts raise their arms in a Nazi salute as they swear allegiance to Adolf Hitler in a mandatory ceremony on October 1, 1936.

government, was turned upside down. A lawyer whose client lied under oath might be held liable for perjury. A judge who failed to perform "in the interests of the National Socialist state," as the Civil Service Act phrased it, could be forced to retire.

The role of the state prosecutor was considerably enhanced, while that of the defense counsel was diminished. The prosecutor took over some of the judge's duties, such as censoring letters written by the accused (even messages to the defense counsel), authorizing prison visits, and dealing with petitions for clemency. Eventually, an official from the Ministry of Justice proclaimed that "since national socialism and justice cannot be separated, there should be no distinction between judge and state prosecutor." Indeed, in some cases the prosecutor actually determined both the verdict—which was usually guilty—and the sentence. Increasingly, the punishment was death. In 1933, only three categories of offense carried the death penalty in Germany; ten years later, there were forty-six such cat-

egories. The nature of the crime, however, was often not the prime consideration; one swindler was sentenced to death because a prior conviction had convinced the court that he would never become a "useful member of the folk community."

Not only were penalties stiffened, but new crimes were conceived. Behavior reflecting lack of enthusiasm for Hitler and the Nazis was declared illegal. The SS and the Gestapo swept people into concentration camps because they looked Jewish or had been denounced by a neighbor or simply seemed suspicious. In one case, a sixty-four-year-old Westphalian woman sitting in a café remarked to her companion, "Mussolini has more political sense in one of his boots than Hitler has in his brain." Five minutes later, the Gestapo, having been telephoned by a patron who overheard the comment, arrived to arrest the hapless woman. In 1932, 250 people had been convicted of sedition; the next year, Hitler's first in power, those sentenced for crimes against the state totaled 9,529.

In 1933, the right of habeas corpus was suspended; henceforth, German citizens could be incarcerated indefinitely without a trial, leaving the Gestapo free to indulge in the favorite tactic of confining people in "protective custody." This method of punishment became so popular that German jails overflowed; authorities had to ease the crowding by conferring blanket amnesties on thousands of short-term prisoners. Frequently, however, prisoners who had been released were rearrested by the secret police and then jailed again.

Hitler himself scorned the German legal system—an attitude he displayed to the fullest at the end of June 1934. Plagued by the demands of the SA, which wanted more power than he intended to give, Hitler purged its unruly leaders. There was no recourse to protective custody or trials for the victims; nor was the action limited to the SA. Nearly 200 people who at some time had offended Hitler or someone close to him were simply taken out and executed. Later, the murders were retroactively legalized by the Reichstag. With the dissidents in his own party silenced, the Reichstag neutralized, and the civil service duly cowed, Hitler by the middle of 1934 held Germany in an iron grip.

The nazification of Northeim did not take that long. By May 1933, one-fifth of the town's adults, 1,200 people, had joined the party. Not everyone joined voluntarily or for motives of personal advancement. Some, such as Otto von der Schulenberg, the county prefect, had little choice. The Nazi county leader, Walter Steineck, threw a swastika pin on Schulenberg's desk and said, "Put that on! If you don't, you won't be prefect tomorrow." Others were pressured, less bluntly but just as effectively, by their own families.

In an early photograph of the concentration camp at Dachau, prisoners loiter outside of their barracks in June of 1933.

Dachau: A Prototype of Evil

Established hurriedly in March of 1933, less than two months after Hitler had come to power, the camp near the Bavarian town of Dachau was initially a makeshift holding pen that was set down amid the stone huts of a disused gunpowder factory. Although it was crude, the camp soon overflowed with 2,000 political prisoners. Some were communists and other militant antagonists of the Nazi regime. Others—guilty of nothing more than opposing Nazi initiatives in the Reichstag—were Socialist Workers, Centrists, Royalists, or representatives of the once-dominant Social Democratic party.

The inmates were systematically humiliated, beaten, worked to exhaustion, and not infrequently murdered by the camp guards. Dachau became a place of dread, a terrifying example of Nazi ruthlessness toward all opponents—and the model for the grisly concentration camps that followed.

Arrivals at Dachau, expressing varying degrees of defiance and apprehension, wait to be processed in May 1933. Held without trial, these so-called enemies of the state had no idea how long their detention would last. "On this account alone," observed a guard, "their life in camp was a torment."

Inmates of Dachau strain to haul a huge roller across the camp's parade ground in 1933. Backbreaking and often pointless labor was a standard feature of life at Dachau and the other concentration camps it spawned.

Jailed Nazi political foes, some of them senior members of the Social Democratic party, gather around a sign that reads, "I am a class-conscious SPD bigwig." Mockery such as this was intended to amuse Dachau's SS guards and degrade the inmates.

One resident remembered wives "who actually went out and bought a brown shirt and put their men into it."

Ernst Girmann moved quickly to take over the town. In preparation for the Reichstag election in March 1933, he redoubled the effort to harass groups and individuals considered to be communist or Marxist. The day after the Reichstag fire in Berlin, February 28, he authorized the town's Storm Troopers to carry fire arms. On the following day, he had thirty SA men sworn in as deputy police officers.

With the opposition parties shackled, Girmann conducted the most intense political campaign that the town of Northeim had seen in its thousand-year history. Radio loudspeakers in the market square blared Hitler's message; uniformed SA, SS, and Hitler Youth marched through the streets; rockets and bonfires lighted the night; and on election Sunday, planes carrying political messages buzzed low overhead. When the onslaught was over, 63 percent of the town's voters supported the National Socialists. One week later, in local elections, the voters elected Girmann and fourteen other Nazis to the twenty-member town council. The remaining five positions went to Social Democrats.

Like Hitler, Girmann was not content with a majority—he wanted absolute, incontestable power. He had an opposing councilman arrested, somehow persuaded another to vote with the Nazis, and harried a third into resigning. He had himself named deputy mayor, made all the appointments to council committees, and refused to allow the Social Democrats even to speak at council meetings. The two remaining dissident members hung on grimly for three months, until a national law dissolved their party and forced them to resign as well. Their replacements were Nazis whom Girmann appointed.

Girmann's next objective was what the Nazis called a "general cleaning action," and it was directed at town employees. Within two months, Girmann had fired forty-five people, one-fourth of the total staff, and replaced them with the party faithful. As was the case at the national level, such replacements scarcely improved the town services. "When the Nazis cleaned out the Health Insurance Office," a local journalist recalled, "they naturally fired the Socialist business manager, a competent fellow. In his place Girmann put a Nazi who had just been released from jail, where he had served a term for embezzlement."

Girmann moved more circumspectly but with no less zeal against the mayor, a courtly civil servant by the name of Peters who had been the town's chief administrator for thirty years. The mayor, an experienced bureaucrat, tried to bend before the winds coursing through Northeim. He applied for membership in the Nazi party and concentrated on balancing

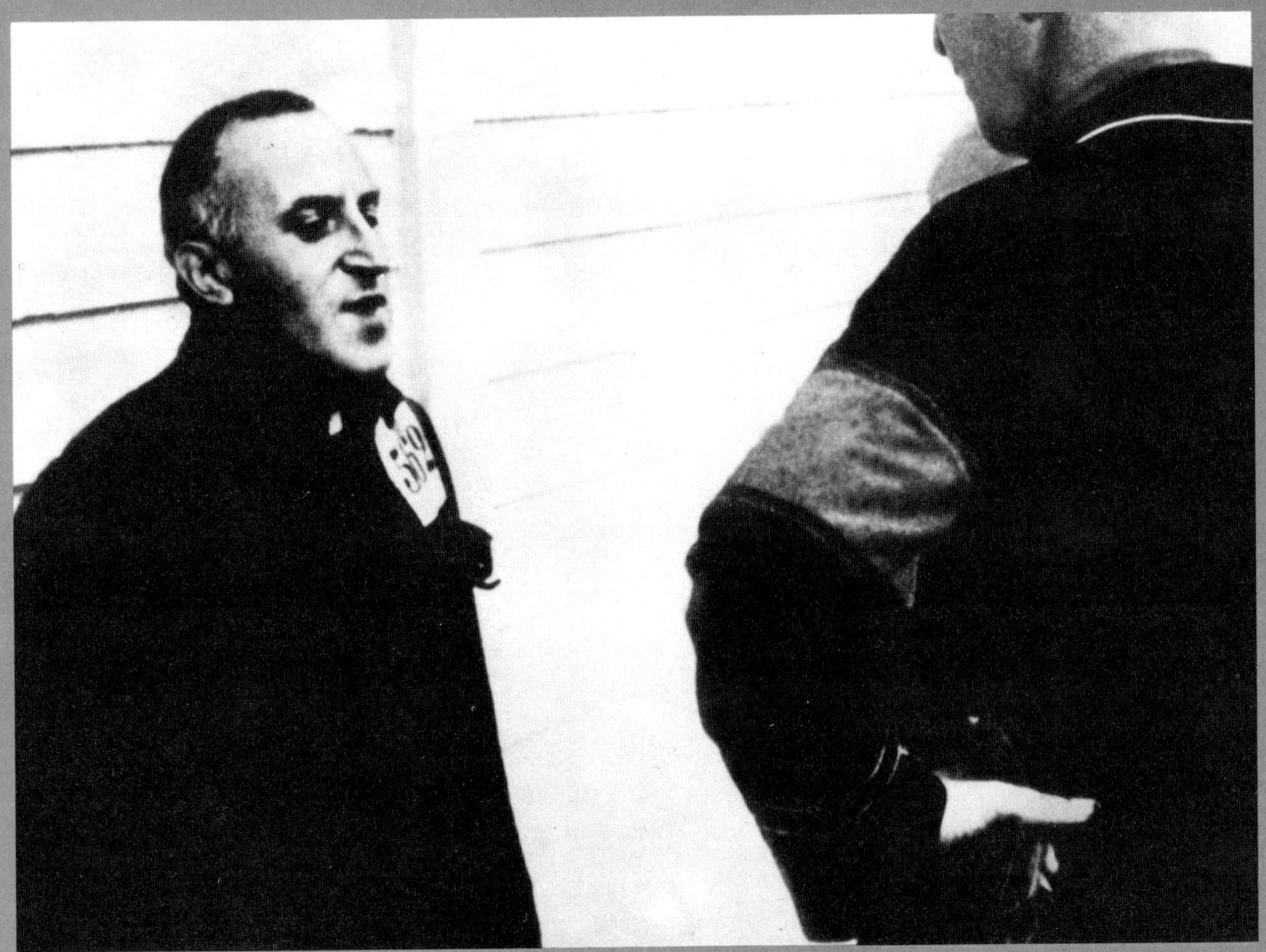

A frail Carl von Ossietzky faces an SS guard at Esterwegen, where the future Nobel laureate was brutalized by his captors.

A Stubborn Voice of Dissent

On November 23, 1936, to Hitler's chagrin, German journalist Carl von Ossietzky was awarded the Nobel Peace Prize. The choice was a stinging rebuke to the Nazi regime. As publisher of the Berlin weekly *Die Weltbühne* in the 1920s, Ossietzky had poured scorn on Hitler and his henchmen. He referred to them as "Adolphus Rex" and his "buffoons" and detected in their rhetoric "a shameless reversal of the simplest definitions of decency and legality."

Ossietzky was equally harsh in his attacks on an institution dear to the Nazi leader, Germany's resurgent military. In 1929, the journalist's exposé on the nation's secret rearmament raised such a stir that he was sent to prison for treason. Released just weeks before Hitler came to power, Ossietzky refused to seek safety in flight. The voice of a dissident in exile, he noted, "soon finds no echo in his own country."

Within months, the Nazis rearrested Ossietzky and eventually consigned him to the Esterwegen concentration camp. There he was tortured, and his health rapidly deteriorated. When his comrades abroad learned of his condition, they mobilized world opinion to save him. In 1934, an exile group, the German League for the Rights of Man, proposed that he be given the Nobel Peace Prize. Luminaries such as physicist Albert Einstein and novelist Thomas Mann endorsed the idea. Hoping to undermine the effort, Nazi propagandists reported that Ossietzky had converted to national socialism. In truth, the ordeal had broken his body but not his spirit. Transferred to a state hospital, he learned that he had won the prize. The government refused to let him accept the award or the money that came with it, however, and Hitler ordered that henceforth the Nobel Prize would not be recognized in the Third Reich.

Ossietzky was moved to another hospital, where he died on May 4, 1938, at the age of forty-eight. In an article written before his arrest, he warned that Germans invited catastrophe by calling on Hitler in their hour of need. "The evil genie," he wrote "is roaring in its bottle."

the town's budget and managing its services while acquiescing in Girmann's exercise of raw power.

The mayor's reward for his forbearance was a smear campaign by Girmann designed to force his resignation. Peters refused to step down at first, but his resistance was in vain. At length, the town council voted a resolution of no confidence in the mayor and announced that there would be no further "collaboration" with him.

Meanwhile, the process of nazification extended to Northeim's every nook. The railroad unions, civil servants' society, craft guilds, and shooting and sports clubs, as well as the organizations of doctors, dentists, and teachers, immediately became targets. Each was taken over by the Nazis or replaced by a parallel Nazi organization and then forced to dissolve. Surviving organizations all had the prefix "National Socialist" added to their names. Even the local Lutherans, confident that their support of the Nazis would bring rewards, found instead that the Nazis intended to take over the churches. The Nazis set out to win Lutheran elective offices and urged the church elders to join the German Christian Movement, a pro-Nazi infiltration group. Even the public library was nazified when 500 volumes of "worthless literary trash" were burned.

The people in Northeim who were not converted or neutralized by nazification were usually subjected to terror. In April, a four-day boycott of the town's Jewish businesses was announced as retaliation against "international Jewry" for "slandering" Germany. The action notified astonished Northeimers that while the Nazis had soft-pedaled their anti-Semitism during the election campaigns, they had no intention of doing so now. Once the point was made, most of the town's 120 Jews submitted to their new role as second-class citizens. And signs appeared in non-Jewish stores that read, "Purely Christian Family Enterprise" and "German Merchant." Later, the signs declared "Jews not admitted."

Non-Jewish Germans were not secure from terror, either. The town police, under Girmann's direction, fanned out to search the houses of anyone thought unreliable and to arrest anyone suspected of disloyalty. This was done with great fanfare, to make sure every citizen was aware that the official knock on the door might come at any time. The local newspaper published a picture of the regime's first concentration camp, at Dachau, and soon reported the establishment of the first such installation in Northeim county, at Moringen, six miles from the town.

To a degree unmatched since the Reign of Terror in France, people were encouraged to curry official favor by informing on their errant friends and neighbors. Students dragooned into the Hitler Youth learned to inform on their teachers and families. People conducted ordinary conversations in

low tones, checked for eavesdroppers, and cautioned each other to be careful, to speak and behave in proper Nazi fashion. The simplest lapse could lead to the loss of a job, the boycott of a business, or a trip to a concentration camp. A doctor who lampooned Hitler at a party was reported to Nazi headquarters the next morning; his hostess had turned him in. "Social life was cut down enormously," said one resident; "you couldn't trust anyone any more."

In Northeim and every other German city, the ominous activities of the Nazi *Blockwart,* or block warden, made people paranoid. The lowest-ranking official in the party, the block warden was charged with the task of keeping tabs on the affairs of forty to sixty households in his neighborhood. On his family data cards he recorded such information as membership in clubs, willingness to contribute money to the party, and evidence of hereditary defects.

The persistence of these domestic spies and their familiarity with their surroundings made them effective snoopers: "It was considerably more difficult to keep a secret from one's block warden, who was obliged to report all his observations, than to mislead the Gestapo," wrote a Nazi official. But the block warden's job was considered a lowly calling, and the position attracted those unfit for other work. One district leader lamented, "We do not have the right men for this extremely important but very difficult task. The majority are aged, bodily handicapped, and intellectually dull and inactive." Less than discriminating, the block wardens produced mountains of information, but little of it proved valuable to the Nazi party. Nevertheless, the overwhelming atmosphere of intimidation that was produced by eavesdroppers and informants, both official and unofficial, dampened the spirit of Nazi opponents everywhere. By the summer of 1933, there was no danger of further resistance from the town administration, the police, the political parties, or any other organization in the town of Northeim. Early in September, Ernst Girmann proclaimed that the revolution was complete, that Germany and Northeim were firmly and irrevocably in the power of the Nazis.

Thereafter, events in the picturesque old town settled into dreary routine. Nazi meetings, rallies, and celebrations continued, and attendance became mandatory. Newspaper notices read, "The *entire* population of Northeim *must* appear!" More acquiescent than enthusiastic, the people complied when they had to, adopted the forms of behavior necessary for survival, and kept to themselves as much as possible.

The Nazis' victory soured quickly in Northeim and across the country. With nothing left to struggle for, the party stagnated. The excitement was over, and functionaries now spent their time mundanely pursuing the

correct use of party titles and combinations of uniform. Bright young Nazi politicians realized that they could better advance their careers in the civil service or the SS, and paying jobs in the party's political organizations were soon filled by those who could not find employment elsewhere. The original activists, disillusioned at the loss of revolutionary fervor, left the party or remained only as nominal members. As one district leader reported, "The Old Fighters are gradually coming to the conclusion that the Nazi revolution has been messed up and the previous successes are being quietly destroyed." By 1935, nearly one-fifth of the pre-1933 leaders had left the Nazi party. On New Year's Day in 1936, Hitler implored the National Socialists to remain a "fanatically sworn community" but assigned his followers nothing to do.

The party bureaucracy continued to grow, creating higher payroll demands. The gauleiters had to step up their efforts to collect from a populace growing heartily tired of frequent fund drives. As much as 25 percent of the party's income came from the sale—mostly through intimidation—of buttons, pamphlets, and subscriptions. One district leader complained that "people did not open the door to political leaders for fear of having to buy something from them."

Amid widespread demoralization in the party, corruption flourished. In 1935, the Reich treasurer exposed 2,350 instances of embezzlement of party funds. Twenty-nine of the political leaders involved committed suicide; the other implicated Nazis received jail terms totaling 573 years. As in other matters, Northeim's experience was typical. Not only did Ernst Girmann receive a handsome salary as group leader and mayor, he played fast and loose with party funds. Donations and dues money disappeared, and unexplained loans to the party accumulated. Girmann's associates received fat city contracts at the same time other business people were strong-armed for contributions.

Northeim's first Nazi, Wilhelm Spannaus, watched these events with growing distaste. He and a handful of his friends—the respectable Nazis of Northeim—endured the violence, racism, and repression in uncomfortable silence, but they could not abide the corruption. As early as December 1932, some of Spannaus's more indignant friends demanded an audit of Girmann's books; for their trouble they were expelled from the party. By the summer of 1933, however, Spannaus could stand no more. Confident of his standing as a senior party member and of the integrity of the upper levels of the Nazi party, he brought numerous charges of corruption against Girmann to the attention of the gauleiter. Spannaus was sure that an investigation would lead to the removal of Girmann and the purification of the local party.

Local Nazi brass strut down the main street of Northeim during a 1937 rally. At far right in the front row marches Ernst Girmann, the early Nazi partisan who had become Northeim's powerful mayor and party chief.

Instead, it was Spannaus, along with his remaining friends in the party, who were summoned to the gau disciplinary committee and charged with conspiracy. All were exonerated—a backhanded admission that their charges against Girmann were true—but nothing was done to rein in the group leader. With his raw power, ruthlessness, and ability to intimidate, he was exactly the kind of man the Nazis wanted in charge of Northeim.

Spannaus remained a member of the party, collecting evidence against Girmann and clinging to the belief that someday the Führer would discover what was occurring and then set things right. The people of the town, in turn, took heart from Spannaus's perseverance. They clung to the belief that once the initial excesses of the takeover had passed, the positive side of national socialism would begin to emerge. They would wait in vain for many disillusioning years. ✚

A Vainglorious Design for the Ages

Nowhere was the Nazi flair for spectacle more rampant than in the mass rallies staged at Nuremberg between 1923 and 1938. The Bavarian city was an ideal site for the huge assemblies. Easily accessible by road and rail, it also boasted a strong party following among its population of 420,000. And because Nuremberg was an imperial city of the Holy Roman Empire—the First Reich—its history inspired the planners of the Third Reich when they set out to create a setting that was suitable for their gargantuan gatherings.

In 1933, Hitler proclaimed Nuremberg the City of Reich Party Congresses, and a 6.5-square-mile area south of town was selected as a permanent rally site. The plan called for stone bleachers that would be supplanted eventually by far-grander structures: a gigantic stadium, a vast Congress Hall for indoor meetings, and an immense parade ground for military exercises.

The chief designer was a talented young architect by the name of Albert Speer, who based his designs on classical models—but on a scale that was unprecedented. "I found Hitler's excitement rising whenever I could show him that, at least in size, we had 'beaten' the other great buildings in history," Speer later wrote.

Had any of the major buildings been completed, they would indeed have dwarfed the great monuments of ancient Egypt and Rome; the stadium alone would have been three times the size of the mighty Pyramid of Khufu. As it turned out, none of the larger structures was finished, even though thousands of laborers worked on the site virtually around the clock from 1933 until the autumn of 1939, when the outbreak of war halted most of the construction. The project's human cost came to light only after the war: At least 30,000 prisoners at nearby concentration camps were worked to death hewing stone for the unfinished monuments to Nazi vanity.

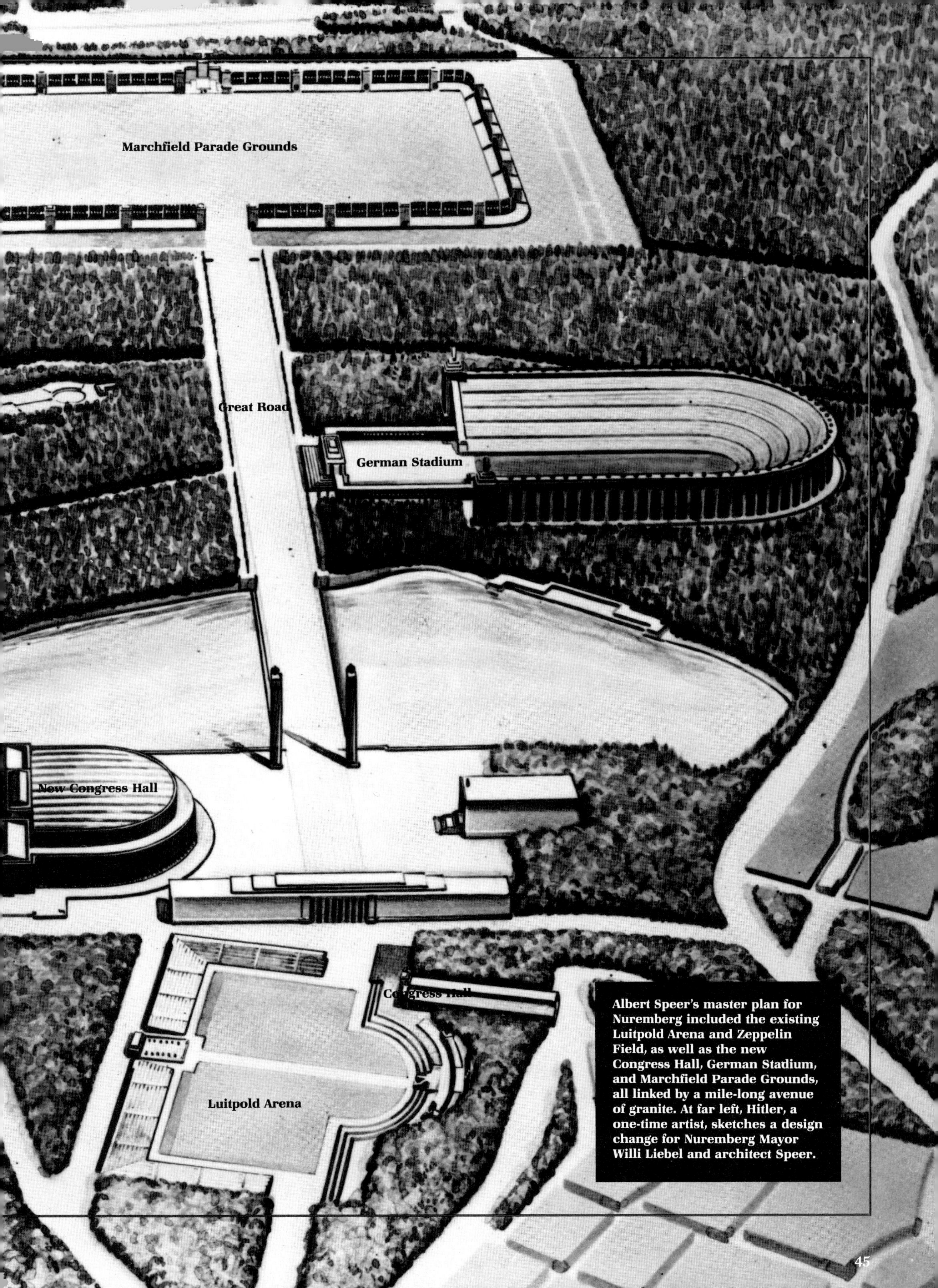

Albert Speer's master plan for Nuremberg included the existing Luitpold Arena and Zeppelin Field, as well as the new Congress Hall, German Stadium, and Marchfield Parade Grounds, all linked by a mile-long avenue of granite. At far left, Hitler, a one-time artist, sketches a design change for Nuremberg Mayor Willi Liebel and architect Speer.

The towering German Stadium, which Hitler envisioned as the permanent home of the Olympic Games, would have been the largest structure of its kind ever built, with seating for 400,000. Its ninety-meter-high rim, taller than Nuremberg's imposing cathedral, was to be studded with massive torches designed from a sketch by Hitler *(inset)*.

Inspired by Rome's Colosseum, the new Congress Hall was designed to seat 50,000 people in its glass-domed central chamber. Work on this temple to fascism—Hitler's favorite building at Nuremberg—continued for two years after the war halted other construction. Yet only the first two tiers projected by the exterior model *(inset)* were completed.

The only one of Speer's Nuremberg designs to be completed, the colonnaded reviewing stand *(inset)* at the Zeppelin Field overlooked a broad plain that could accommodate 250,000 participants. For the Nazis' 1934 rally, Speer encompassed the field with 130 antiaircraft searchlights to create an effect he described as a "cathedral of light." The glow could be seen as far as Frankfurt, [illegible] miles away.

TWO

Masters of Manipulation

The movie begins with a grand sweep of sky. From mountains of billowing white clouds, a silver airplane breaks into the clear. Below, a panorama unfolds as the camera tracks across the historic towers and spires of a medieval city, Nuremberg. The plane's shadow passes over a column of marching men in brown shirts. Other streets appear, each filled with goose-stepping columns. At length, the airplane lands and taxies to a halt. From its gleaming hull, like a deity descended from the heavens, emerges the Führer, Adolf Hitler. A cheering throng surges forward to greet him.

This sequence, taken from the celebrated propaganda film *Triumph of the Will,* illustrates the opening moments of the Nazi party congress of September 1934, which drew 1.5 million Germans to Nuremberg. Such mass assemblies, with their torchlight processions, searchlights stabbing the night sky, rousing speeches, and chanted choruses of "Sieg heil!" were a vital part of Germany's new order. By participating either directly in the pageantry and ritual or vicariously via radio and motion pictures, millions of Germans absorbed the intended message: Under its indomitable Führer, the Third Reich grows strong and unified. In Hitler's exalted thrall, the citizens of Germany could rise above the harsh reality of life in a country strangled by depression. "People complain extensively about conditions," said a report smuggled out of Germany in 1935 by opponents of the regime, "but they shout the loudest when they are fired with enthusiasm by Nazi speakers at some rally or other."

"Propaganda," wrote Joseph Goebbels, "has absolutely nothing to do with truth." Here, his image reflected in a tabletop, he sits under a portrait of Hitler, who called him "my faithful, unshakable, shield bearer."

Besides staging uplifting public events and distributing inspirational films, Nazi propaganda bureaus found other ways to beguile the public. The photographic and artistic image, the printed and spoken word, the sounds of music—all became instruments for supplementing intimidation and terror in the regime's massive effort to control the minds, emotions, and behavior of everyone in the Third Reich. To be sure, the manipulation of public and private opinion had been practiced by myriad rulers, despotic and benevolent, long before the National Socialists took over Germany in 1933. But no government had ever set out to enchain every means of expression as systematically as the Nazis did.

Although Hitler was the true genius of Nazi propaganda, he delegated day-to-day authority for its dissemination to the gifted disciple who liked to be called "Herr Doktor"—Paul Joseph Goebbels. An energetic little man who stood scarcely five feet tall and weighed just a bit more than 100 pounds, Goebbels had big eyes, a diabolical grin, and a talent for distortion, half-truth, and outright prevarication. For the benefit of future propagandists, Goebbels cynically summed up the essence of his craft: "Any lie, frequently repeated, will gradually gain acceptance."

Goebbels's cynicism grew from a seedbed of bitterness and self-hate. He was born in 1897 into a devout Catholic family in Rheydt, a textile center in the Rhineland. His thrifty father, a clerk in a lampwick factory, recorded in a blue ledger everything his family spent, and young Joseph came to detest the watchful pfennig-pinching and tight morals of the lower middle class.

He also hated his own body. Besides being so small, he had a permanent limp—the result of a crippling childhood disease (probably polio- or osteomyelitis) that left one leg three inches shorter than the other. After this handicap had caused him to be rejected for front-line duty in World War I, he concocted a tale that the limp was the result of a wound suffered on the battlefield. And although he excelled in his studies and received a doctorate in German literature from Heidelberg University in 1922, Goebbels got nowhere in his ambition to become a professional writer. Publishers rejected his novel and turned down his plays, poems, and most of his newspaper articles.

In their Sunday best, young Joseph Goebbels and his brother Hans are spruced up for confirmation in the Catholic church. From all evidence, Joseph and his two brothers had doting parents and a warm, harmonious home life.

In 1924, Goebbels found his calling. He went to work as an editor for a newsletter published by the right-wing alliance that included the Nazi party. Soon he became an assistant to Gregor Strasser, a former pharmacist who was the Nazis' chief organizer and Hitler's ideological rival in the party. While serving Strasser, Goebbels discovered to his delight that he had a special gift for public speaking. When he was "a preacher, an apostle, a crier of battle," he wrote, "the soul of the German worker is in my hands, and I can feel that it is soft as wax." He proved so adept at manipulating an audience that he caught the attention of Hitler,

A teenage Goebbels, his hands clasped, is surrounded by his upper-school classmates in Rheydt, his hometown northwest of Cologne. A gifted student, he excelled in Latin and religion, but his arrogance made him unpopular with his peers.

who launched a campaign to woo him away from Strasser. Goebbels had recently denigrated Hitler as "petit bourgeois" and demanded his expulsion from the party. But in time, he came under Hitler's spell and, in his diary, gushingly professed his admiration for the Führer.

Hitler made the twenty-nine-year-old Goebbels the party's gauleiter in Berlin and lectured him on the crucial importance of propaganda. The Führer had been a practitioner of the art since 1919, when he took his first postwar job as an army political-education officer for the 1st Bavarian Rifle Regiment. He had been impressed by the work of British propagandists during World War I. He was convinced, in fact, that the British barrage of words and pictures, which attributed fictitious atrocities to the Hun, had decidedly undermined the morale of German soldiers and civilians. From this lesson, Hitler wrote in *Mein Kampf,* he had learned that propaganda "must always be addressed to the masses" and "must confine itself to a very few points and repeat them endlessly." Hitler also took from the erstwhile enemy the maxim "Tell a lie, and it sticks."

Encouraged by Hitler's tutelage and driven by the need to revive the fractious, anemic party organization in Berlin, Goebbels blossomed into a tireless and inventive propagandist. He developed eye-catching posters, published simple pamphlets with such titles as *The Little ABCs for National*

His clubfoot evident, Goebbels arrives at work in Berlin, where as Nazi gauleiter during the 1920s he led his outnumbered followers against the Communists in a violent contest for political domination. "We must cease to be anonymous," he told his men. "Let them curse us, libel us, battle and beat us up, but let them talk about us!"

Goebbels was a master orator with a rich voice, meticulous timing, and a full range of gestures, as the sequence above shows. He practiced his delivery for hours at a time before a three-sided mirror, and to good effect: Hitler said Goebbels was the only speaker he could listen to without falling asleep.

Socialists, and started a Nazi weekly newspaper, *Der Angriff* (The attack), that specialized in vicious caricatures of Jews and Marxists. He provoked brawls with communists and then propped up his own wounded and heavily bandaged Storm Troopers to show them off as martyrs at party rallies. He disrupted the premiere of the American-made antiwar film *All Quiet on the Western Front* by releasing white mice and harmless snakes in the theater. He made a heroic myth of the sordid story of Horst Wessel, a young Storm Trooper who had been killed by a communist—the former suitor of Wessel's prostitute girlfriend. And he elevated a primitive marching song written by Wessel into the anthem of the Nazi movement. No propaganda was "too crude, too low, too brutal," Goebbels announced, as long as it was successful in getting attention or winning converts. "The people want to be bamboozled."

In 1930, Hitler promoted Goebbels to party propaganda chief, a post the Führer himself had been filling. While retaining the job as party leader of Berlin, Goebbels took a prominent role in subsequent Nazi election campaigns, nurturing the myth of Hitler as a messianic redeemer who would save Germany from the Jews and Marxists. Goebbels eventually expressed this myth in terms of an ear-catching trinity: *ein Volk, ein Reich, ein Führer* —one people, one nation, one leader.

Goebbels was rewarded for good service on March 13, 1933, six weeks after Hitler had become chancellor. He was appointed to Hitler's cabinet in the new position of minister of popular enlightenment and propaganda. The ministry consolidated functions formerly scattered in a half-dozen government agencies, and it assumed sweeping new powers. By decree, Goebbels was to be responsible "for all influences on the intellectual life of the nation; for public relations for state, culture, and the economy; and for the administration of all the institutions serving these purposes."

Goebbels pursued his assignment with ruthless energy. He established his new ministry, which came to be known as Promi, in an old palace on the Wilhelmplatz. When civil servants failed to redecorate the offices promptly enough to suit him, he sent in a crew of Storm Troopers to rip out the plaster and tear down the old wood paneling. With similar decisiveness, he raided other ministries and party offices to staff Promi. At the age of thirty-five, he was the youngest and one of the best-educated cabinet ministers in all of Europe, and he wanted bright, young subordinates. Many of his recruits were so inexperienced in government he had to bring in a veteran civil servant from the Finance Ministry to lecture them on the ways of the bureaucracy. They learned quickly, for Goebbels was soon demanding that memos reaching his desk contain plain diction and consist of no more than five typewritten pages.

Although Promi grew rapidly and soon expanded to thirty-two regional offices, Goebbels wanted to extend his domain even further to embrace all of German cultural life. Scarcely six months after his appointment to the cabinet, he persuaded Hitler to create a new agency, the Reich Chamber of Culture. The chamber consisted of seven components—for literature, theater, music, film, fine arts, the press, and broadcasting. Everyone who "produced, distributed, or sold cultural property"—newsstand operators as well as reporters, theater managers as well as film directors—was required to join the appropriate chamber and submit to the dictates of the chamber president, Goebbels. These Nazi licensing bodies excluded Jews, other non-Aryans, and anyone deemed politically unreliable, none of whom were allowed to practice their professions, since they did not belong to the chamber.

Der Stürmer
Deutsches Wochenblatt zum Kampfe um die Wahrheit
HERAUSGEBER: JULIUS STREICHER
Schriftleitung und Verlag: Nürnberg-A, Pfannenschmiedsgasse 19
Zu beziehen durch jede Postanstalt oder direkt durch den Verl

Vor 2000 Jahr

hetzten an allen Orten des rö
reiches jüdische Propagandisten
Mittelmeeres zur

Weltrevol

auf. Sie verkündeten die F
und erklärten, nun wü
Herrschaft üb
antreten. Dieser jüdisch
Revolutionspropagan

Chr

mit seinen Lehren
den ganzen Haß
auf sich. Die Jud
es schließlich
Golgatha sein
Tode versucht

An advertisement for a special Easter edition of the newspaper *Der Stürmer* in 1937 depicts a sinister Jewish visage presiding over the Crucifixion. The virulently anti-Semitic weekly, published by Julius Streicher *(right)*, was so scabrous it embarrassed even the top Nazis; nevertheless, the paper had a circulation of 700,000 and made Streicher a multimillionaire.

Armed with his three separate but interlocking directorates—Promi, the Reich Chamber of Culture, and the party propaganda office—Goebbels set

out to shackle the communications and cultural media of the Third Reich. His most formidable target was the press, which was both voluminous and diverse. When the Nazis came to power, German publishers were producing 7,000 magazines and journals and 4,700 daily and weekly newspapers—more than any nation in the world.

These newspapers and periodicals represented many different special interests, including religions, trade unions, and political parties of every stripe. In February of 1933, the burning of the Reichstag, which Hitler blamed on the Communists, provided a rationale for the suppression of left-wing newspapers—both Communist and Social Democratic. But the newspapers controlled by the Nazis still constituted less than three percent of those remaining, and they performed so poorly that Goebbels confided to his diary, "We have the best speakers in the world, but we lack nimble and skillful pens."

The regime tried to harness the vast number of evenhanded newspapers—those that presented the news without pronounced political bias—and to force them to hew to the Nazi line. Late in 1933, Goebbels combined into one official state-owned agency the two existing wire services that gathered news at home and abroad and disseminated it to the press. This agency, the German News Bureau (DNB), provided as many as 60,000 words a day, more than enough to fill a newspaper's columns. The DNB came under the direction of Promi and thus gave Goebbels control of much of the news at its source.

Another maneuver enabled Goebbels to curb the press by restraining newspaper editors. The Editors' Law of October 1933 removed editors from the traditional control of newspaper publishers and thrust them squarely under the heel of the state. Editors were made personally responsible for every word printed in their newspapers and forbidden to publish material that was considered potentially damaging to the Reich. Moreover, editors could work at their trade only if their names appeared on a so-called professional roster maintained by Promi. Names could be struck from the roster, thus costing editors any chance to pursue their livelihood, for transgressions as slight as drawing a distinction between Germans and Austrians after the Anschluss in 1938. In the words of the official commentary to the law, an editor was a "state organ who is called upon to fulfill one of the most important tasks of the state."

Having regimented the news through the DNB and forced editors to censor themselves, Goebbels established an additional control. During the Weimar Republic, government representa-

tives had answered journalists' questions at daily press conferences. Goebbels now converted this forum into a platform for telling reporters precisely how to do their job. Every day at noon and, after the war broke out, at a second conference held in the evening, one of Goebbels's deputies presented the audience of several hundred correspondents with oral comments and written directives known as "language rulings." The ministry considered these directives confidential; the journalists, who represented both the big-city dailies and the provincial press, had to sign affidavits swearing that, after reading these voluminous instructions, they would destroy them in the presence of a witness.

The directives, which were crammed on a dozen or so typed yellow sheets, told reporters everything the regime wanted them to know about the day's news. The guidelines detailed what stories to publish and what pages to run them on, how to slant articles, and even how large to make their headlines. "From 1933 onward," recalled a journalist, "editors more and more became simply rubber stamps for officially stated views, placing their mark on the daily copy to indicate that they had worked on the material, and nothing more." Even Goebbels admitted privately that "any person with the slightest spark of honor left in him will take good care in the future not to become a journalist."

The directives covered every nuance of the party line. A typical issue, from April 1935, banned photographs showing government leaders before rows of bottles at banquets. "The utterly absurd impression has been created among the public," it explained, "that members of the government are living it up." No one was to refer to beggars or poor children without mentioning the charities operated by the Nazi party. In May 1938, just before the bloodless conquest of Czechoslovakia, the press was ordered to "make a big thing of any incidents" caused by Czechs along the border. In November 1938, following *Kristallnacht,* the virulent episode of physical assaults on Jews and their shops and synagogues, a directive baldly ordered newspapers to deemphasize the wanton destruction and violence and play up the "people's indignation" against Jews. Even the classified ads were fair game: Goebbels warned newspapers not to accept notices seeking housemaids for childless households because the regime's family policy encouraged having as many children as possible.

Goebbels took umbrage at stories that revealed the secrets of his propaganda machine and how it stage-managed the news that Germans received. Shortly after World War II broke out, he erupted in anger when an illustrated magazine published a picture of a radio technician playing the phonograph record that produced the fanfare preceding special battlefield communiqués. Goebbels appeared at a press conference and threatened

Relaxing at his desk, the Führer peruses the *Völkischer Beobachter,* the official Nazi party organ that became Germany's first national newspaper. Published simultaneously in Munich, Vienna, and Berlin, it attained a circulation of 1.2 million readers by 1941.

to jail anyone who committed the crime of "exposing the illusion in any nationally important procedures."

In preparing press directives, Goebbels and his minions were seldom hampered by considerations of accuracy and truth. General Instruction No. 674, which was issued in late August of 1939, presented a dilemma because it had to go to the printer for reproduction and subsequent distribution to the press only a few hours before it was clear whether Hitler had decided to invade Poland. Promi covered both contingencies nicely by wording the directive in the following manner: "In the next issue there must be a lead article, featured as prominently as possible, in which the decision of the Führer, no matter what it is, will be discussed as the only correct one for Germany."

To enforce the directives, a nationwide network of press wardens monitored local newspapers by carefully reading each edition and reporting any transgressions. Failure to follow press directives, or the commission of other sins, brought swift punishment that varied in severity. In 1936, an embarrassingly frank headline in Berlin's *8 Uhr Abendblatt*—"An additional billion taxation revenue required"—resulted only in confiscation of that edition of the paper. But mentioning a forbidden name—a once-prominent socialist, for example, or a Jewish author—usually cost the responsible editor his job. Other offenders might be jailed. The editor and the publisher of an Essen newspaper were sent to a concentration camp for a composing-room error that many readers found hilarious: A caption describing a carnival appeared under the picture of a solemn procession of Nazi Storm Troopers.

Awesome as it was, Goebbels's power over the press failed to render him omnipotent. In the propaganda fiefdom, as in other realms of the Nazi regime, Hitler maintained a policy of divide and rule, protecting his own position atop the hierarchy by establishing conflicting authority among his deputies. Thus while Goebbels regimented the press, another Nazi chieftain worked with Hitler's blessing to bring more and more newspapers under the ownership of the party.

The overlord of the Nazi press and Goebbels's bitter rival was Max Amann—also of dwarflike stature and physically handicapped: He had lost his left arm in a hunting mishap. Amann was the director general of the Munich-based Eher Verlag, the party's official publishing house, which put out such books as *Mein Kampf* and such newspapers as *Völkischer Beobachter* (People's observer). His friendship with Hitler dated to the Great War, in which he had served as company sergeant in the Führer's unit. In 1921, Hitler had appointed Amann business manager of the party and, the following year, head of Eher Verlag.

A billboard advertising Hitler's magnum opus, *Mein Kampf*, during German Book Week in 1934 is underscored by his self-endorsement: "I read endlessly and thoroughly. Within a few years, I had created a base of knowledge that I still tap today."

Amann was in many ways a strange choice. He was talented at neither writing nor public speaking, was largely indifferent to Nazi ideology, and possessed a brutal temper under his jovial Bavarian exterior. But he was a shrewd businessman with a knack for hiring gifted subordinates. He transformed the newspaper from a struggling weekly into a prosperous daily that eventually would attain a circulation of more than one million

Max Amann *(left)* rides in a military parade with Robert Ley, director of the German Labor Front, and their wives. Hitler called Amann, publisher of the paper *Völkischer Beobachter* and head of a Nazi publishing empire, "the greatest newspaper proprietor in the world."

in separate editions printed in Munich, Berlin, and Vienna. Much of the party organ's success stemmed from the Nazis' rising fortunes, of course, and after the takeover, many people subscribed to it out of self-protection. Nonetheless, Hitler held Amann in high regard. He even made Amann his personal banker, entrusting Eher Verlag with stewardship of the royalties earned from *Mein Kampf,* which in 1933 alone amounted to the equivalent of $300,000. When the most prominent author in Germany needed money, he simply phoned Amann.

Amann and Goebbels first clashed during the autumn of 1933 over the Editors' Law, which reduced the power of publishers, including those who were Nazis. Goebbels prevailed on that issue, but he was unable to shrink his rival's expanding empire. Amann maintained his close relationship with the Führer, and Goebbels was one of Amann's authors at Eher Verlag; the high-living propaganda minister could not push too hard lest he jeopardize his badly needed cash advances.

In the party and government, Amann gradually acquired power that enabled him to bring many more newspapers into the National Socialist fold. First, as Hitler's designated Reich press leader, a party post, he consolidated under Eher Verlag scores of local Nazi papers that had previously been controlled by the gauleiters. At the same time, a number of Jewish publishers were forced to sell out to Eher at a fraction of their worth after the government ordered publication suspended or applied other pressure, such as boycotting those who advertised in the offending newspapers. Among the victims was the Ullstein Verlag, a large family-owned corporation that published books, magazines, and three of the leading Berlin dailies. "Now we have bought the largest German publishing house," Amann boasted after completing the Ullstein purchase in 1934, "and it has not cost us as much as a pencil."

It was after Amann had been appointed president of the Reich Chamber of the Press—one of the components of the Reich Chamber of Culture—that he achieved his greatest acquisitions. On April 24, 1935, Amann handed down ordinances that crippled much of the remaining privately owned press. These ordinances required publishers to prove their German ancestry to the year 1800, gave Amann the right to close or suspend newspapers in areas of the country where too much competition made publishing economically unfeasible, and prohibited individuals from owning more than one newspaper. The mere suggestion that a newspaper might be shut down under the broad interpretation of one of these far-reaching ordinances prompted more than 500 publishers to either fold or sell out to Amann's Eher Verlag.

As a result of Amann's maneuvers, by 1939 the number of German newspapers had shrunk by more than one-half. Eher Verlag, which had accounted for only 2.5 percent of all newspaper circulation in 1932, now openly or secretly controlled at least 66 percent. During wartime, by exploiting government-imposed sanctions on newsprint, the Nazi party's domination of circulation would grow to 82.5 percent. Eher's profits approached those of even Germany's largest corporation, the enormous I. G. Farben chemical combine. Amann shared in these profits shamelessly, largely through his secret one-third holding in the printing company that handled much of the Eher Verlag's business; during the decade after Hitler had taken power, Amann's annual income increased from about $43,000 to more than $1.5 million.

Nazi ownership of some papers and the censorship of others made the German press less readable and less appealing to its audience. Goebbels had envisioned the medium as an orchestra in which each instrument played the same melody—the party line—but with a different tone and

Underground Humor with a Bite

For many Germans, humor was the best tonic for coping with everyday frustrations, and poking fun at ranking Nazis became a popular pastime. Open ridicule, such as the cartoon of Joseph Goebbels at left, created in 1934 by anti-Nazi émigrés, could be published with impunity only outside the Reich.

At home, mockery was at least slightly subtler and included a verbal shorthand in which abbreviations had special meanings. A "Goeb," for Goebbels, was the widest a mouth could be opened without splitting it or the least energy needed to silence 100,000 radio receivers. A "Ley," for Robert Ley, was the longest a person could talk gibberish nonstop, and a "Gör," for Hermann Göring, was the most medals a man could pin to his chest without falling on his face.

The economy, the bureaucracy, and even the party were fair game for such barbs, but the Führer was not. Most Germans approved of Hitler, and vignettes about him tended to skirt his foibles and tout his superiority and craftiness. Anyone who indulged in less flattering depictions usually made the mistake only once; anti-Hitler jokes were punishable by death.

expression. Instead, the system resulted in parrotlike papers so dull and uniform that they lost one million readers in 1934 alone. To rekindle lost interest, Goebbels and his deputies periodically admonished journalists to avoid the tired clichés of nazism and become more inventive. On one occasion, Goebbels tried to introduce variety into the coverage of a story by ordering several newspapers to emphasize different aspects of it—an attempt that only called attention to his regimentation of the press.

In order to relieve the one-note tedium, Goebbels permitted a few highly respected papers to continue publication with a modicum of editorial independence. He tolerated one relatively liberal newspaper, the *Frankfurter Zeitung*, largely because of its international reputation. The paper's continued presence—without the Jewish family who had owned it since the year 1856—lent prestige to Hitler's regime and gave Goebbels a vehicle for influencing public opinion abroad. So long as the newspaper toed the line on foreign policy, it was allowed freedom to comment on some cultural and religious matters.

The *Frankfurter Zeitung's* editors accepted this limited independence because they felt certain Hitler shared their goal of a strong but peaceful Germany. They failed to discern that the regime had been lying to them all along, and when Hitler's troops invaded Poland on September 1, 1939, the editor in chief, Rudolf Kircher, was shocked. He collapsed in hysterical sobs. His newspaper, the last vestige of journalistic freedom in Germany, survived until 1943 before Hitler ordered it closed.

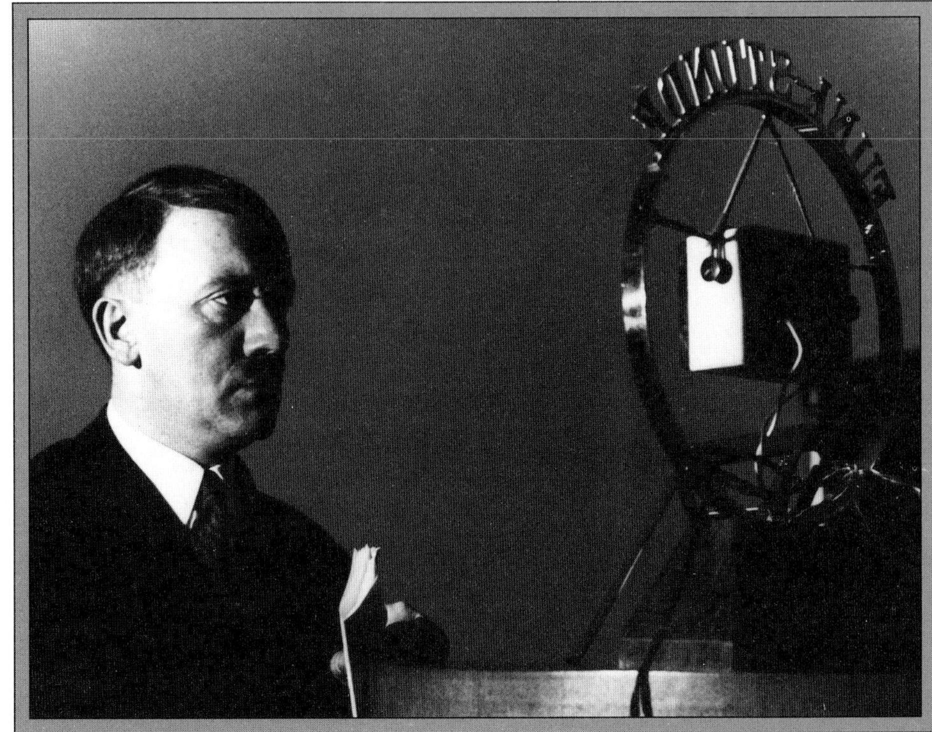

As propaganda instruments, Goebbels preferred the two newest forms of mass communication—radio and film—over the old-fashioned press. The rapid growth of home radio ownership during the late 1920s and the advent of talking pictures had coincided with the emergence of the Nazi party. Both forms also appealed to Hitler, who liked the spoken more

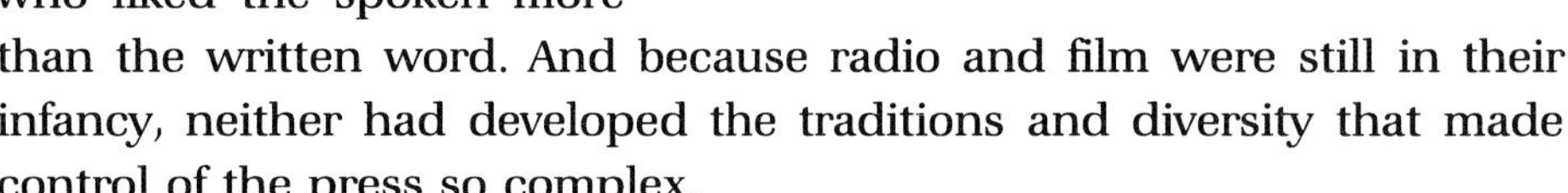

than the written word. And because radio and film were still in their infancy, neither had developed the traditions and diversity that made control of the press so complex.

Goebbels regarded radio as the most effective manipulator of public opinion. The German broadcasting system had been in government hands since its inception in 1925, and the propaganda chief took advantage of it from Hitler's first day as chancellor. During 1933, the Führer broadcast forty-five speeches to the nation. It was immediately apparent, however, that Hitler could conjure up what he called the "magic of the spoken word" only on a platform before an audience. In a studio, he spoke too rapidly and garbled his words. Unlike the newly elected president of the United States, Franklin Roosevelt, who was a master of the intimate fireside chat, Hitler needed the direct rapport of an adoring throng, with its rhythmic applause and rapturous chants. Goebbels made sure the Führer had an audience for all subsequent broadcasts.

In March 1933, Promi took over the German broadcasting system, absorbing its national transmitting center and all regional and local stations. Goebbels's agents replaced the existing staff with so many of the party faithful that one old hand noted in his diary that his station resembled a Nazi barracks. Two months later, he was fired for being a Social Democrat

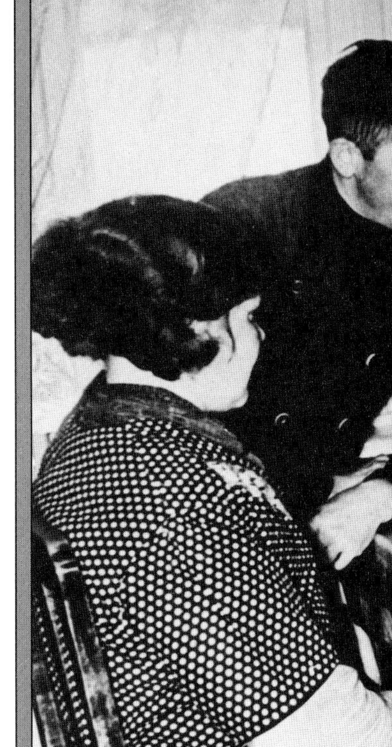

and having a Jewish wife. To create the largest-possible audience, Promi pressured manufacturers to produce an inexpensive radio—the *Volksempfänger,* or people's receiver. It sold for seventy-six reichsmarks, or about thirty dollars, less than the price of a good suit of clothes. An even cheaper version—with sufficient power to receive only domestic broadcasts—sold for less than half that much. Between 1933 and 1939, radio ownership tripled. Seventy percent of German homes had at least one radio—the highest household saturation of any country in the world.

The regime also encouraged communal listening. In the belief that broadcasts would carry a greater impact when heard in groups, Goebbels had radio loudspeakers installed on city streets and ordered that factories, stores, offices, beer halls, and other public places be equipped with large receivers. During programs deemed important by Promi, work and other activity came to a halt so everyone could gather around the radio. Thousands of neighborhood radio wardens working for the party organized group listening, monitored programming preferences, and dutifully reported the barrage of complaints whenever local stations devoted too much time to National Socialist political broadcasts.

Keenly aware of radio's propaganda potential, Hitler timorously learns to speak into a studio microphone. Below, members of a rural family listen to the Führer's message on their inexpensive *Volksempfänger,* or people's receiver.

After the broadcasting schedule had evolved, about one-fourth of the nineteen hours of daily programming comprised commentary, speeches, and drama intended as straight propaganda. The rest was news (from the government-owned DNB, the same agency that served the press) and music. At first, heavy symphonic works dominated the Nazi airwaves, but room was soon made among the Beethoven and Wagner for light opera, marches, waltzes, and folk music. Goebbels realized that he needed entertainment to keep listeners tuned in for the propaganda messages. "At all costs, avoid being boring!" he advised a group of broadcasters. He watched programming closely and often immersed himself in petty details. For example, he directed a station in Vienna not to get on the nerves of listeners at ten o'clock in the morning with what he called "your all-too-fruity Viennese band music."

If Goebbels liked to dabble in radio, he was obsessed by film. An "impassioned devotee of cinematic art," as he described himself, he main-

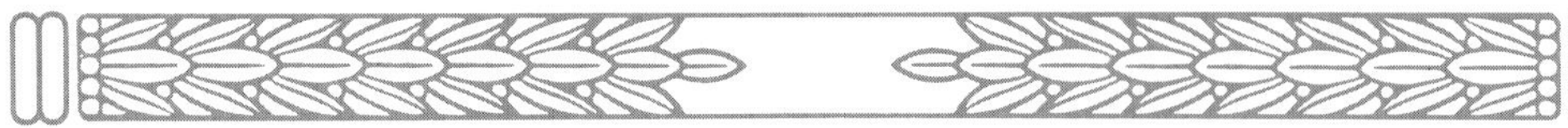

tained private screening rooms in each of his three homes and found time to see at least one film a day even on his busiest days. He loved film for its intellectual content and for the emotional appeal that made it a dynamic medium for propaganda. One of his favorite movies was *Gone with the Wind.* He also repeatedly viewed such officially forbidden films as *All Quiet on the Western Front,* the antiwar classic whose premiere he had sabotaged in 1930, because it was a "very clever propaganda vehicle."

The minister regretted the mass exodus of movie talent following the Nazi takeover—even though the exiles were objectionable in the eyes of the Nazis. The German film industry had been renowned for its originality and creativity, but scores of its best people—among them the director Joseph von Sternberg and performers Peter Lorre and Marlene Dietrich—left for Hollywood and other film capitals because they were Jews or political liberals. Goebbels tried to persuade Fritz Lang, director of the widely acclaimed *Metropolis,* to make movies for the Nazis even though he came from Jewish ancestry. Lang asked for twenty-four hours to think it over. Then he hurriedly had a friend book a berth for him on the train to Paris and fled Berlin that very night. A Jewish actor named Leo Reuss pulled off another kind of exit. He went to Vienna, dyed his hair and beard blond, and—to the praise of Nazi film critics—specialized in so-called Aryan roles in Austrian movies. At length, Reuss merrily revealed his identity and headed to Hollywood to work for Metro-Goldwyn-Mayer.

To prevent others from joining the exodus, Goebbels initially granted more creative freedom to filmmakers than to editors and broadcasters. But before long he abandoned all pretense of artistic freedom and assumed nearly absolute authority over the movie industry. Through Promi and the Reich Chamber of the Cinema, he approved all scripts, decided which projects were entitled to government financing or tax breaks because they were "politically and artistically especially valuable," and approved and

A poster for the anti-Semitic movie *Jud Süss* shows the Jewish villain Süss peering menacingly from under bushy brows. The script, in which Süss extorts, tortures, and rapes, was so depraved that Goebbels had to browbeat a director and actor into making the film.

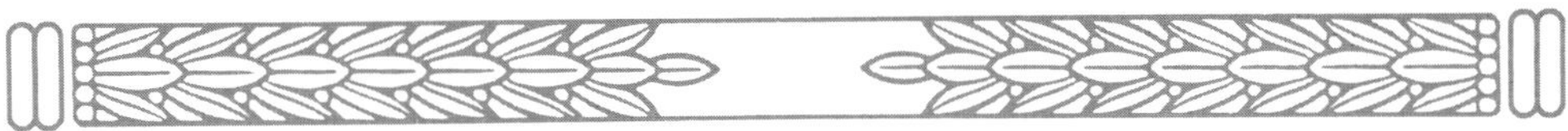

censored films. He became even more powerful—and intrusive—after Promi took ownership of the four major film studios in 1937. He intervened in cast selection, ordered directors to reshoot entire scenes that displeased him, and, it was said, previewed every film made in the Reich, from educational shorts to full-length features.

By and large, the films that emerged from this tightly controlled apparatus were surprisingly free of overt Nazi messages. The most blatantly propagandistic were the documentaries, the newsreels shown weekly in theaters and the party-produced shorts on Hitler Youth and other Nazi themes carried in the 1,500 mobile vans that introduced cinema to rural Germany. A handful of feature films made early in the regime, such as *SA-Mann Brand* and *Hans Westmar* (a retelling of the Horst Wessel legend), glorified the Brownshirts. But Goebbels changed his tactics after lagging box-office returns demonstrated that the Storm Trooper's place is, as he put it, "in the streets and not on the screen."

Goebbels thereafter tried to give moviegoers refuge from the flag waving and Hitler saluting of everyday life. Of the 100 or so feature films produced annually, only about one-fourth carried a discernible propaganda message; in these films, the Nazi line was often immersed in the subtleties of dramas involving historical figures. The eighteenth-century Prussian ruler Frederick the Great, for example, was a favorite of German filmmakers. For their message films, Nazi studios also leaned toward biographies of such German achievers as the poet Friedrich Schiller, who—like Hitler, it was implied—exemplified the triumph of untutored genius over formal learning. But most feature films were a benign mixed bag of comedies, adventures, romances, and frothy musicals. Escapist fare, Goebbels hoped, would lure viewers to the theater, where they would be forced to watch the propaganda-laden newsreel. Audiences were literally trapped in some cases, because after 1941 theater doors were commonly locked during the showing of the newsreel. Not incidentally, the patrons' box-office contributions held down the film-industry deficit, which ranged from $4 million to $6 million each year.

As war approached, Goebbels stepped up the tempo of pure propaganda. In 1938, after Hitler had complained about the scarcity of movies with Nazi themes, Goebbels ordered the production of several scurrilous anti-Semitic films. One of these, *Jud Süss,* was loosely based on an actual incident. The movie depicted an evil eighteenth-century Jewish financier who is condemned to death after an uprising of the people. Members of the cast, concerned that perhaps they had been too convincing, asked Promi to publicize that they were not actually Jewish but simply good actors. In any event, the film was evidently realistic enough to prepare

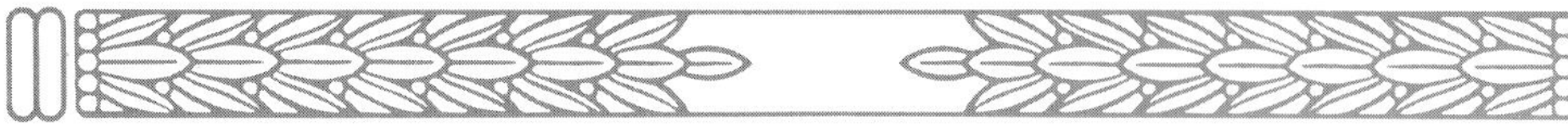

public opinion for future atrocities: Some teenagers who saw it became so incensed that they beat up Jews afterward.

Goebbels meddled in the production of this film and many others. When an early studio version of *Jud Süss* presented a proud martyr rather than a cringing villain, Goebbels ordered extensive reshooting and editing. He and other Nazi censors rejected Tarzan films imported from the United States because the hero and his mate were too scantily clad. The officials also discouraged adultery in domestic movies because it detracted from the Nazi emphasis on family and prolific —but legitimate—procreation. But when members of the army high command objected to a film in which a famous singer allowed a pilot to spend the night with her, the Luftwaffe chief, Hermann Göring, intervened on the side of artistic license. "The man would not be an officer," he announced, "if he did not take advantage of such an opportunity."

Hitler entertains Goebbels, his wife Magda, and three of their children—Hilde *(left)*, Helmut, and Helga—at Berchtesgaden in 1938. The Führer considered the Goebbelses an ideal German family and spent much of his free time in their company.

Despite his public stance as a bluenose, Goebbels in private was an energetic womanizer. Perhaps dazzled by his position of power, women found him attractive despite his short stature and physical deformity. He spoke with a sonorous baritone, had slender and expressive hands, and cut an intriguing figure in the elegantly tailored white gabardine suits that contrasted with his naturally swarthy skin, which he further darkened with a sunlamp. Since his youth, Goebbels seemed to have always felt the need to prove himself with women. "Eros speaks to me with a powerful voice," he once wrote in his diary. His

post as film potentate gave him access to a glamorous galaxy of established actresses and ambitious starlets. He seized the opportunity and carried on frequent and open liaisons at his two country villas, his palatial house in Berlin, and even his elegantly appointed private offices at Promi.

Goebbels's attractive wife, Magda, was aware of this double life and did not object so long as his affairs remained mere dalliances. Perhaps because she took an occasional lover of her own, and certainly because of the Goebbelses' close friendship with Hitler, she was willing to maintain the fiction that she and her husband were the regime's model couple. Hitler had been a witness at their wedding in 1931, and he took a special interest in their growing family, which produced six children by 1940. He happily let the children call him "Uncle Adolf" and even "Uncle Führer."

Then one of Goebbels's dalliances turned into a grand passion that threatened the marriage. In 1936, he met and fell in love with Lida Baarova, a twenty-two-year-old film star who had moved to Germany from her native Czechoslovakia. The affair had raged for two years and become the talk of Berlin before word finally reached Hitler in the summer of 1938. The Führer, fearful of a scandal that would stain his government, summoned his errant minister. Not only were the rumors true, Goebbels confessed, but he wanted to divorce Magda, resign his position, and go abroad with Baarova, perhaps as ambassador to Japan. Hitler furiously replied that it was all out of the question, and Goebbels quickly caved in to his beloved Führer. After one last tearful telephone conversation with Baarova, he agreed that she be sent back to Czechoslovakia. Goebbels then made sure that her latest film was removed from all the theaters in the Reich.

Goebbels's affair with the Czech actress Lida Baarova, shown here in a publicity photo, almost cost him his marriage and his career. The Nazi minister was a notorious skirt chaser: "Every woman quickens my blood," he wrote in his diary. "I run around like a hungry wolf."

Goebbels evidently never attempted a romance with the most glamorous and talented figure in the Nazi film industry, Leni Riefenstahl. In fact, the two were highly competitive; Goebbels disliked and may have even feared Riefenstahl, who produced and directed two extraordinary documentaries, *Triumph of the Will* *(next pages)* and *Olympia.* With her healthy good looks and clinging white gowns, she cut a wide swath through the Berlin party circuit, usually on the arm of some high-ranking Nazi—occasionally the Führer himself. When she and the propaganda minister crossed paths at parties, both well tanned and in white, they flashed movie-star grins and then privately grumbled about each other.

The precocious daughter of a Berlin plumber, Riefen-

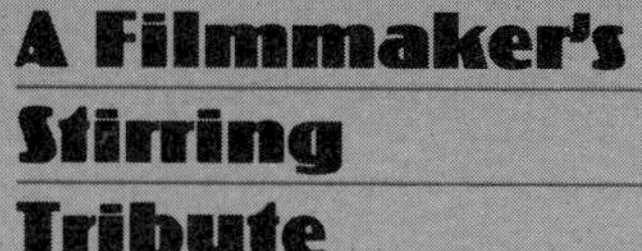

A Filmmaker's Stirring Tribute

Leni Riefenstahl's *Triumph of the Will,* glorifying Hitler and the 1934 Nuremberg party rally, was acclaimed the world over as the most powerful documentary ever made. The black-and-white film featured dramatic lighting, unusual camera angles, a dazzling juxtaposition of images, and a stirring score.

In editing the film, Riefenstahl cut from medieval buildings to a floodlit German eagle to the faces of young Nazis. Mingling the nation's history with its rebirth under Hitler, she combined shots of flags, massed ranks of the faithful in the huge Nuremberg stadium, and marching SS men. Again and again, the brilliant and politically savvy filmmaker returned to closeups of the Führer, as he entranced the crowd with his oratory.

A gracious Führer receives a curtsy from the Norwegian figure-skating champion Sonja Henie during the 1936 Winter Olympics, which were held in the twin villages of Garmisch-Partenkirchen in the Bavarian Alps. The Nazi regime prepared unrivaled facilities for the games, including the outdoor rink *(left)* where Henie won her third Olympic gold medal.

stahl started as a ballerina but made her film debut in 1925 at the age of eighteen. She played in so-called mountain films, a unique German genre that pitted strong young men and athletic women against the Alpine heights. In 1931, when she was not yet twenty-five years old, Riefenstahl formed her own production company and co-authored, directed, and starred in *The Blue Light,* a poetic mountain drama that won a gold medal at the Venice Biennale the following year.

The image of a heroic skier adorns this poster commemorating the 1936 Winter Games, which the Germans produced as a successful dress rehearsal for the Summer Olympics in Berlin.

In 1932, Riefenstahl became involved in one of Goebbels's periodic campaigns to fix up the Führer with an attractive woman. Goebbels and his wife hosted a dinner one evening in their Berlin apartment and invited Riefenstahl and Hitler. Another guest, Ernst "Putzi" Hanfstaengl, the Nazis' Harvard-educated foreign press chief, later recounted that after dinner the filmmaker invited everyone to her studio. Hanfstaengl, as was his custom on such occasions, provided soft background music at the piano—like a pianist at a house of ill repute, he later remarked.

"Riefenstahl was certainly giving Hitler the works," he wrote. "There she was, dancing to my music at his elbow, a real summer sale of femininity." Hanfstaengl and the Goebbelses slipped discreetly away to allow romance to take its course. But when Hanfstaengl saw Riefenstahl a few days later, she answered his unspoken question with a negative shrug of the shoulders. She insisted after the war that "Hitler respected me as an artist, nothing more."

Hitler respected Riefenstahl so much that, besides serving as her occasional escort, he made her his personal filmmaker. Her initial major commission was to film the Nazi party congress at Nuremberg in September 1934. The Nuremberg rally was a red-letter day in the busy calendar of events orchestrated by Goebbels to foster feelings of national community, mass euphoria, and adulation for the Führer. First staged in that medieval city in 1923 in order to generate the illusion of a link between nazism and early German history, the rally combined routine meetings of Nazi party organizations with a spectacular show of well-rehearsed mass pageantry and quasi-religious ritual influenced in part by Goebbels's and Hitler's Catholic boyhoods. The 1934 rally was to be the greatest gathering yet, involving far more than a million participants and spectators. Hitler and Goebbels considered the week-long

A Victor in Sport and Combat

Wreathed in laurel, Lieutenant Gotthard Handrick *(center)* savors victory at the 1936 Olympic Games in Berlin.

Lieutenant Gotthard Handrick of the Luftwaffe's Richthofen Squadron fulfilled a Nazi propagandist's dreams. An outstanding athlete as well as a skilled pilot, Handrick emerged as a shining exemplar of the new Germany at the 1936 Olympic Games in Berlin, where he won the pentathlon, a grueling test that involves horseback riding, fencing, shooting, swimming, and running. The versatile lieutenant could do no wrong; a journalist who revealed that Handrick had drunk a liter of beer a few hours before the shooting contest praised the drinking as a "calculated move" by a master competitor who knew when to key himself up—and when to relax.

Within a year of his victory at the Olympics, Handrick's nerve was tested anew, this time in combat, as he led a German fighter group against the Spanish loyalists. Returning from his tour of duty in Spain, he received a hero's welcome in Berlin, having shot down five enemy airplanes in a Messerschmitt 109 that had been aptly decorated by his mechanics *(right)*.

Handrick's plane bears Olympic rings.

festival to be an especially crucial demonstration of solidarity after the recent purge and murder of the Storm Trooper chief Ernst Röhm and other high-ranking National Socialists.

To Goebbels's consternation, much of the 1934 show was shaped to suit Riefenstahl. First the Führer commissioned the documentary without consulting Goebbels. Then Hitler ordered Goebbels's ministry to finance the movie, script the rally in large part to fit Riefenstahl's needs, and keep hands off the finished product.

Goebbels's ego may have suffered, but not the Nazi propaganda effort. In *Triumph of the Will*—a title bestowed by Hitler—Riefenstahl produced a masterpiece of propaganda and film technique, a paean to the Führer. Working with thirty cameras and a staff of 120 technicians, she borrowed from the techniques of the Russian director Sergey Eisenstein to create dramatic backlit closeups, low-angle shots, and other novel images. From her old mountain films, she retained the technique of creating panoramas of massive forms, but now the granite cliffs and the clouds were replaced by enormous aggregations of Nazi party members. In the editing room, she compressed and rearranged the images in order to further transfigure reality and glorify the Führer.

Two years later, Riefenstahl applied her talent to an even more ambitious event, the 1936 Olympic Games in Berlin. The result was *Olympia,* which premiered in April 1938 to mark Hitler's forty-ninth birthday. Less blatantly political than *Triumph of the Will,* the film nonetheless propounded such Nazi themes as the cult of virile health and worship of the human body. Hitler praised it as a "unique and incomparable glorification of the strength and beauty of our party," even though the film's undeniable star was Jesse Owens, the black American sprinter and jumper who won four gold medals but no congratulations from the racist Führer.

In addition to controlling the mass media, the Nazis wanted to make culture itself the servant of the Reich and party. In their view, literature, theater, music, and the fine arts should hew to an ideology that rejected rationalism and the intellectuals who espoused it. Hitler expressed his distaste for intellectuals in an interview with Berlin's foreign press corps in 1938. "Unfortunately, one needs them," he lamented. "Otherwise, one might—I don't know—wipe them out or something."

Central to this antirationalism and key to the party line on culture was the mystical Nazi vision of the *Volk,* or racially pure German people. "We want to lead art once again to the people," said Goebbels in veiled doublespeak, "in order to be in a position to lead the people once again to art." He and other party luminaries saw no need for meddlesome cultural critics to intervene between the people and the works of art approved by the party. Julius Streicher, publisher of the scabrous *Der Stürmer* and gauleiter of Franconia, was once so outraged by newspaper reviews of a variety show that he dragged the critics to the theater and forced them to sing and walk a tightrope in front of the performers. In 1936, Goebbels went a step further and simply banned all criticism of the arts. "Articles on the arts will describe rather than evaluate," he announced. "They will give the public the opportunity to make its own judgment."

In all his decisions concerning propaganda and censorship, Goebbels had to defer, of course, to the opinions of his Führer. He also had to contend with the meddling and tedious pedantry—"philosophical belching," he called it—of Alfred Rosenberg, the semiofficial ideologist of the Nazi party and Goebbels's main rival in the regimentation of the arts. Although Rosenberg and Goebbels agreed in principle about National Socialist goals, they differed sharply in their methods. Goebbels, a wily pragmatist, was willing to compromise ideology, if necessary, in order to win the hearts and minds of the German people. In contrast, Rosenberg was strict and unyielding in his interpretation of Nazi dogma and uncompromising in his effort to enforce the party line.

Goebbels maliciously referred to his rival as "Almost Rosenberg" because he had "managed to become a scholar, a journalist, a politician—almost." Rosenberg, born in 1893 in Estonia to a shoemaker of German ancestry, took a degree in architecture from the University of Moscow, then fled to Germany after the Russian Revolution of 1917. He became one of Hitler's first mentors in anti-Semitism and served as editor of the Nazi newspaper *Völkischer Beobachter.* In 1929, he established within the party the Fighting League for German Culture to counter modern tendencies in arts and letters. Five years later, Hitler, as part of his divide-and-rule game, further augmented Rosenberg's authority by appointing him the party's supervisor for "intellectual and ideological training and education."

It was in the realm of literature that Rosenberg posed his strongest challenge to Goebbels's control of culture. Within weeks after Hitler had been appointed chancellor, pressure from Rosenberg's fighting league forced the ouster of nearly half the members of the Literature Section of the prestigious Prussian Academy of Arts; among those writers expelled or made to resign was the Nobel Prize-winning author Thomas Mann. On May 10, 1933, young militants, egged on by the rabble-rousing of Rosenberg and other ideologues, staged a mammoth book burning in Berlin *(next pages)* that destroyed the works of Freud, Marx, and scores of others—an act that would be repeated throughout Germany that spring. Goebbels appeared at the bonfire in Berlin to praise the "strong, great, and symbolic act," but

In the library of a Berlin hostel, a member of the *Studentenbund*, the Nazi student association, gathers books for burning.

An Orgy of Book Burning

The most repelling of early Nazi demonstrations was the conflagration of books that lighted the heart of the city of Berlin on a May night in 1933, less than five months after Adolf Hitler had taken power. Thousands of German students, screaming slogans about fighting "decadence and moral decay," hurled more than 20,000 volumes into a single, enormous bonfire.

No branch of the government orchestrated the book burning—although Joseph Goebbels attended and gave a suitably aggressive speech. Rather, the students themselves organized the destruction. Inflamed by Nazi propaganda reviling all left-wing authors, intellectuals in general and Jewish ones in particular, militant Nazis among Berlin University's student body spent weeks compiling lists of "un-German" writers and books, then ransacking both public and private libraries for the offending volumes. On May 10, the students hauled their huge take in trucks and carts to a city square that was bordered, ironically enough, by the campus of the venerable university and the proud Berlin State Opera House. There they put the so-called decadent books to the torch.

Though not directly involved in the burning, the Nazi hierarchy enthusiastically approved. Within weeks, similar bonfires flared at thirty other German universities and in hundreds of towns. The books destroyed included works by some of Germany's greatest thinkers, such as Albert Einstein and Thomas Mann, and by an eclectic assortment of writers from other countries *(page 81)* who had in common only their belief in the dignity of the free human spirit.

Sanctioning the book burning by his presence, Joseph Goebbels lauds the arsonists for destroying intellectualism and other "unworthy filth."

Undergraduates, some wearing SA uniforms, convoy a truckload of books to the fire. Their sign reads, "German students march against the un-German spirit."

Shouting denunciations of "cultural decadence" and all "false ideas of freedom," student leaders pitch books onto the roaring pyre.

Writers whose books were burned in Berlin:

Henri Barbusse
Franz Boas
John Dos Passos
Albert Einstein
Lion Feuchtwanger
Friedrich Förster
Sigmund Freud
John Galsworthy
André Gide
Ernst Glaeser
Maxim Gorki
Werner Hegemann
Ernest Hemingway
Erich Kästner
Helen Keller
Jack London
Emil Ludwig
Heinrich Mann
Thomas Mann
Karl Marx
Marcel Proust
Erich Maria Remarque
Margaret Sanger
Arthur Schnitzler
Upton Sinclair
Kurt Tucholsky
H. G. Wells
Theodor Wolff
Émile Zola
Arnold Zweig

more out of duty than conviction; book banning, not burning, was his style. These events, dark portents for artistic freedom in Germany, triggered an exodus from the country that eventually totaled more than 2,500 writers who feared for their work—or for their lives.

Goebbels subsequently faced competition from a plethora of would-be censors within the Nazi party. Rosenberg took on an additional bureau in this field, the Reich Office for the Promotion of German Literature. Soon he oversaw a staff of 1,400 readers, who turned out evaluations of 10,000 books a year—half of all the titles published in the Reich. In 1933, twenty-one different offices in the party and government became involved in the suppression of books. Gradually, however, Goebbels outflanked Rosenberg and other rivals, largely on account of his superior strength in the government as both propaganda minister and president of the Reich Chamber of Culture. Hitler, for his part, preferred Goebbels's practicality to Rosenberg's strident and uncompromising dogma. Indeed, the Führer once referred to his ideologist as a "narrow-minded Baltic German who thinks in horribly complicated terms."

By the summer of 1935, Goebbels had an exclusive stranglehold on authors, publishers, libraries, and bookstores. His Reich Office of Literature, a Promi agency, became the regime's sole censor of books. His Reich Chamber of Literature, in addition to maintaining the register of approved writers, issued a regular index of "harmful and undesirable literature"—old and new, German and foreign.

Now that a centralized apparatus was in place, the Third Reich could get on with the business of blacklisting books. More than 12,400 titles were decreed contraband and made subject to confiscation by agents of the Gestapo. At the same time, Goebbels's agencies promoted novels and nonfiction works that extolled the familiar Nazi themes of martial virtue, racial purity, and the mystique of the peasant. None of these volumes, however, approached the popularity of the Führer's own turgid contribution to German literature, the book *Mein Kampf*, which sold more than six million copies during the 1930s.

Regulation of the theater, in contrast to literature, followed an erratic course. In censoring the theater, Goebbels had to contend with another party rival, Hermann Göring, who married an actress and considered the Prussian State Theater his private preserve. A more important factor was Goebbels's own indifference; the propaganda minister preferred to spend his spare hours involved in cinema. He did find time to promote a theatrical innovation called *Thing*, taking the Old German name for an open-air people's assembly. Staged in specially designed outdoor amphitheaters, *Thing* productions featured historical pageants that were intended to express and engender feelings of national community. But *Thing,* with its large groups of actors marching back and forth and speaking their lines in unison, soon proved to be an embarrassment—artistically and at the box office—and it died out.

Goebbels admitted that what remained for theater audiences—"classics on the one hand and harmless trivialities on the other"—left something to be desired. He presumably placed in the latter class the clumsy Storm Trooper genre—which someone later described as the "literature of the goose step"—and rustic comedies about life on the farm. In 1934, the play that received the Berlin Critics' Prize, and the admiration of Hitler, featured as its protagonist a pig.

A replica of a Viking ship moves along a Munich boulevard on July 26, 1937, in a pageant celebrating the opening of the new House of German Art, which looms in the background. In a speech dedicating the museum, Adolf Hitler condemned modern artists as "miserable unfortunates who clearly suffer from defects of vision."

Sepp Hilz, an officially sanctioned artist, works with a model to create *Rustic Venus*. Hitler approved of painted nudes, so long as they exhibited what he saw as ideal Nordic racial traits and a virginal wholesomeness.

In the realms of music and the fine arts, the Führer's ironclad opinions reigned supreme. He venerated Richard Wagner and claimed to have seen some of his operas more than 100 times. Indeed, Hitler never missed the annual festival at Bayreuth that was devoted to the nineteenth-century romantic composer. The Führer also tolerated the light operas of Richard Strauss, one of the composers who remained in Germany and even served as first president of the Reich Chamber of Music. But many others fled as Hitler rejected the music of Mendelssohn, Mahler, and other classical composers of Jewish ancestry, as well as any form of dissonance, including jazz. The music of the leading contemporary composer in Germany, Paul Hindemith, ran afoul of the Nazi regime on three different counts: He had worked with Jewish musicians, experimented with dissonance, and once wrote an opera in which a woman appeared nude in her bath. Hindemith left the country in 1938.

Hitler similarly adopted an unrelenting stand against modernism in art. A one-time aspirant to the prestigious Viennese Academy of Fine Arts, he rejected expressionism and surrealism as the work of "cultural cave men, aesthetic dwarfs, and artistic stutterers." Hitler wanted a new people's art that glorified the healthy, the strong, and the heroic. This would be achieved through a literal realism in which the grass was always green, the sky blue, and the plowed furrows of precious German soil so precisely rendered that the viewer could count each one. Those artists whose work failed to live up to the Führer's vision faced sanctions that might include cutting off their supply of materials from the local art shop. Those ordered to cease painting could expect the Gestapo to raid their homes to see whether their brushes were wet.

The Führer's favorite painter was Adolf Ziegler, a comrade from the early days of the Nazi party. Hitler commissioned Ziegler to paint a portrait of his niece, Geli Raubal, the great love of the Führer's life. Technically proficient but uninspired, Ziegler specialized in pseudo-classical nudes with such names as *The Goddess of Art*. At Hitler's behest, Goebbels in 1936 appointed Ziegler to preside over the Reich Chamber of Art, whose 42,000 members included not only painters and sculptors but architects, interior decorators, and landscape gardeners.

In 1937, Hitler and Goebbels entrusted to Ziegler the additional task of purging the museums and galleries in the Third Reich. Under Ziegler's orders, the National Socialists confiscated some 16,000 pieces of so-called degenerate art, including works by such giants as Max Ernst, Paul Klee, Wassily Kandinsky, Vincent van Gogh, and Pablo Picasso. Hundreds of pieces were sold on the international market in order to obtain foreign currency for the regime; others were appropriated for the private collec-

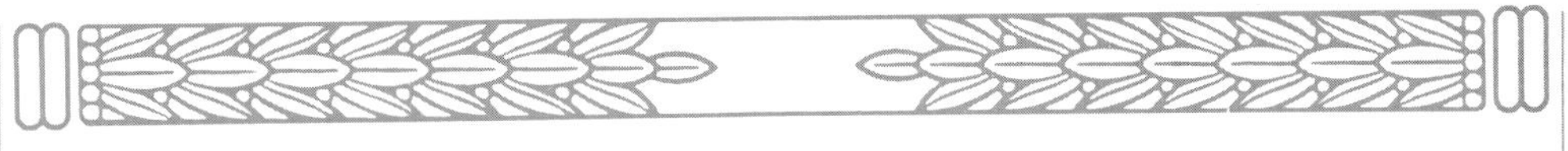

tions of Göring and fellow Nazi bigwigs. Much of the remaining confiscated art went into storage. But in 1939 the Nazis announced that they needed the warehouse space to store grain for wartime, so they heaped 4,829 paintings, prints, and drawings in a huge pile in the courtyard of Berlin's main fire station and set them aflame.

Before the Nazi haul was sold, stolen, and burned, however, Goebbels had Ziegler organize an extraordinary display of works selected from the collection. This Exhibition of Degenerate Art, which opened in the city of Munich in July of 1937, featured some 730 pieces created by Germans such as Emil Nolde, Max Beckmann, and others and such non-Germans as Marc Chagall and Piet Mondrian. The paintings were purposely displayed in a jumble without frames, and they were hung under lurid headings such as "Thus is nature seen by sick minds" and "The Jewish yearning for desolation comes out." To the dismay of the National Socialists, the show was the most popular display of paintings ever staged in the Third Reich, attracting two million visitors—five times the number that visited the concurrent exhibition of approved art, which was also held in Munich. It was never clear how many of the visitors came to see the "degenerate" show as a protest and to take one final look at great art that was earmarked for oblivion, or how many merely wanted to confirm their own prejudices against modern art and demonstrate their agreement with the new cultural establishment.

Similarly, it was difficult to measure with precision the effects of the Nazi regime's continuous campaign of propaganda and cultural regimentation. Certainly, many Germans were confused and troubled by what was happening in their country. Some sought alternative sources of information and tuned in the British Broadcasting Corporation and other foreign broadcasts before the practice was outlawed with the outbreak of war. Others took refuge in cynicism. A worker in Hamburg said, "I told my old lady that if I die, don't let them put it into the newspaper, because no one will believe it." Many German citizens simply stopped reading and listening and withdrew into apathy—not necessarily because they disagreed with what Goebbels told them, but because they needed to protect their innermost selves from the incessant barrage of propaganda.

But the image of the Führer penetrated even the protective shells of apathy. His picture stared down from walls everywhere, and his name

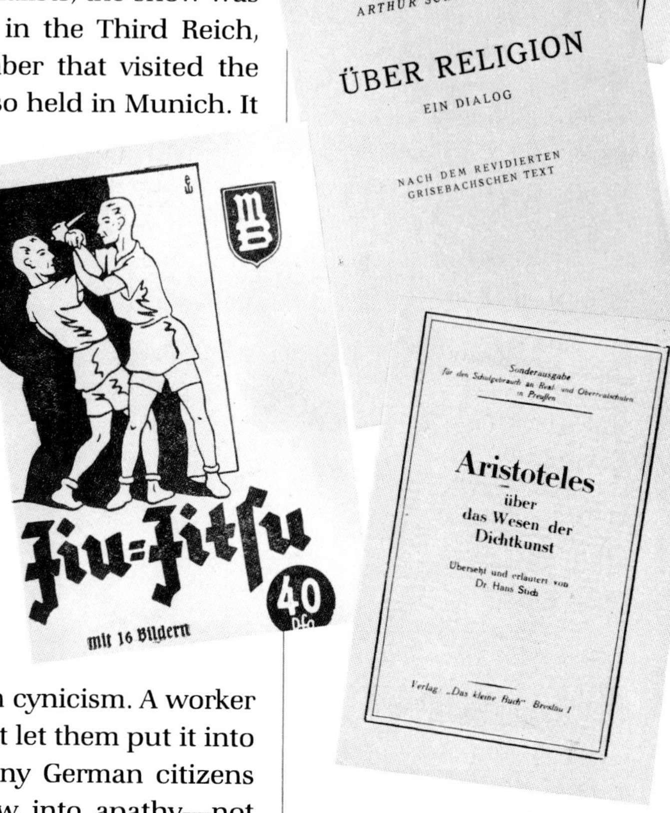

Innocuous pamphlet covers, claiming to represent works by historical figures, instead conceal anti-Nazi propaganda. Such revolutionary messages were circulated by resistance groups that operated clandestinely inside Germany.

A photomontage by the German artist John Heartfield portrays a symbolic victim of nazism draped across a swastika, a concept inspired by the medieval torture device that was known as the wheel. Heartfield, a communist who had gone into exile in 1932, smuggled his anti-Nazi images back into Germany from Czechoslovakia.

resounded in the ubiquitous greeting, "Heil Hitler!" Clearly, by 1939 the massive effort to win the people's hearts and minds for the Führer had achieved a high degree of success. However they felt about national socialism, Germans fervently believed in the myth of the Führer. They attributed to him the Reich's rising prosperity and renewed strength and prestige, and they blamed his underlings, including the propaganda minister, for anything that went wrong.

So intense was the faith in the Führer to set things right that thousands of German citizens wrote to him with their suggestions and complaints. The writers received in reply only a preprinted card, which informed them that their letters had been forwarded to the appropriate authorities. Few of the correspondents ever heard anything more from this regime that so rarely found itself at a loss for words. ✚

A German eagle clutches a swastika above the five-ring Olympic insignia on this medal, which was awarded to organizers of the 1936 Berlin games.

Director Leni Riefenstahl offers hands-on guidance to one of her cameramen covering the competition in Berlin. Riefenstahl shot a million feet of film and spent eighteen months editing her epic documentary, *Olympia*.

A Triumph of Propaganda

The right to stage the Olympic Games was an honor that Hitler did nothing to earn and everything to exploit. As the accused aggressors in the Great War, Germans had been barred from the quadrennial competition in 1920 and 1924. But early in 1931, two years before the Nazis took power, the International Olympic Committee awarded the 1936 summer games to Berlin as a signal that Germany was once again considered a responsible player in the diplomatic arena. At the time, Hitler denounced the proposed Olympics as a charade and said they "cannot possibly be put on in a Reich ruled by National Socialists." Once installed as chancellor, however, he recognized the games as an unparalleled opportunity to promote his regime. By 1935, the British ambassador to Germany noted that Hitler was growing obsessed with the coming event: "He is beginning to regard political questions very much from the angle of their effect on the games."

Hitler had reason to be concerned with the impact of politics on his Olympics. The regime's blatant anti-Semitism and aggressive rearmament—underscored by the remilitarization of the Rhineland in March 1936—led the major Allied powers and other countries to consider boycotting the games. Nazi officials countered by proclaiming their peaceful intentions and allowing a few individuals of mixed Jewish ancestry to contribute to the Olympic effort. In the end, France, Britain, and the United States joined fifty-two nations in sending teams to Berlin.

Encouraged by the Allies' capitulation, Hitler and Propaganda Minister Goebbels went further in their efforts to disarm critics of the Reich. Anti-Semitic signs and newspapers were removed from view in Berlin during the games, and books the Nazis had banned or burned mysteriously reappeared on bookstore shelves.

The regime's most dramatic diversion was launched far from home. On July 20, 1936, a runner at the site of the ancient games in Greece began the first Olympic torch relay. Documented by filmmaker Leni Riefenstahl *(right)*, the relay involved more than 3,000 participants. They carried the flame symbolizing the spirit of friendly competition northwestward through the Balkans to the Reich. Not many years later, German panzers would follow the path in reverse.

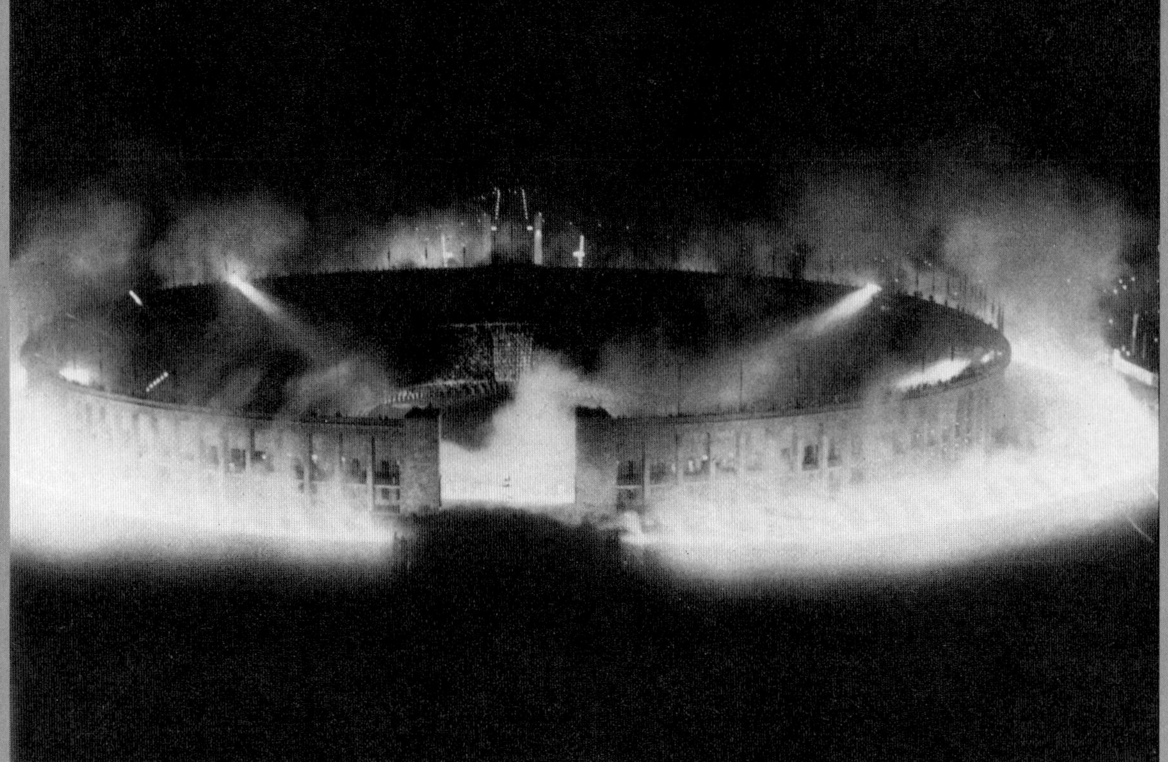

Searchlights illumine the 110,000-seat Olympic Stadium on the games' first night.

Flaunting the Torch of Nationalism

As the hand-carried Olympic torch neared Germany for the games' opening ceremonies, the flame ceased to be a symbol of international goodwill and became an object of Nazi pride. The passing of the torch through Vienna sparked an outburst by 10,000 Austrian Nazis. They shouted Hitler's name and chanted, *Deutschland über alles!* Once the torch reached German soil, the demonstrations became more orderly but no less partisan; thousands of members of the Nazi party and the Hitler Youth lined the way, hailing the runners as though they were conquering heros.

Berlin, meanwhile, was dressing up to receive the flame. The route from the center of the capital to the new Olympic Stadium *(above)* was festooned with national flags, Olympic insignia, and stark swastikas. "The whole town was a thrilling pageantry of royal banners," wrote the visiting American novelist Thomas Wolfe, who marveled at flags "fifty feet in height, such as might have graced the battle tent of some great emperor."

On the morning of August 1, as the final torchbearer loped toward the Olympic site, the 803-foot-long dirigible *Hindenburg*, a soaring emblem of German pride, cruised overhead. As the runner entered the stadium to ignite the beacon at the far end of the field, tens of thousands raised their arms in stiff salute *(right)*. A short time later, a German weightlifter stepped to the podium and, while grasping a Nazi flag, administered the Olympic oath to the assembled athletes.

Garbed in summer whites, members of the Hitler Youth salute flaxen-haired Fritz Schilgen, a middle-distance runner, as he carries the Olympic torch into the stadium to open the 1936 games.

Diversions for the Masses

Like the rulers of ancient Rome, who staged lavish spectacles to placate the restless masses, Hitler and his aides used the Berlin Olympics to divert attention from the harsher aspects of life in Nazi Germany. Besides the events on the playing fields, there were innumerable sideshows to distract the public.

The biggest stir was created by Hitler himself, who presided in cordial grandeur from his box at the Olympic Stadium *(left)*. Outside the arena, thousands of doting Germans who had descended on Berlin without tickets, milled about, hoping to catch a glimpse of Hitler's passing motorcade.

Notables from abroad enjoyed closer contact with Nazi luminaries at garden parties, where doubts about the regime were allayed by smiling hostesses and free-flowing champagne. Among the Americans to share in the festivities were aviator Charles Lindbergh and swimmer Eleanor Holm Jarrett *(right)*, who had been dismissed from the United States' Olympic team for drinking. The Nazis did their best to keep the glamorous Holm in the limelight, aware that the scandal would preoccupy the potentially troublesome American press corps. In the end, such tactics succeeded. Beguiled by the bread and circuses in Berlin, most foreigners did not stop for a hard look at their hosts.

Adolf Hitler and Joseph Goebbels *(far left)*, who were stars in their own right, sign autographs at the Olympic Stadium.

Eleanor Holm Jarrett, world recordholder in the backstroke, manages a smile despite being kicked off the United States' team. Holm boasted of training "on champagne and caviar."

A Setback for Aryan Supremacy

The Berlin games sorely tested the Nazi theory of Aryan supremacy. That doctrine had seldom been challenged in Hitler's Germany, where non-Aryans were excluded from most athletic clubs and events. When a prominent Jew in Württemberg committed suicide after being barred from the sports club he had organized, Nazi gauleiter Julius Streicher exulted, insisting that there was "no place for Jews" in German sports. Streicher also canceled wrestling matches between German challengers and a black champion, explaining that he would not let "white men be subdued by a black man."

Such incidents might have derailed the Berlin Olympics had Hitler not appeased foreign critics of his anti-Semitic policies by such token gestures as allowing fencer Helene Mayer *(top right)* and organizer Theodor Lewald *(bottom right)* to participate in the games. Aryan supremacists could rationalize the success of Mayer and Lewald by noting that they were only partly Jewish, but the racists were at a loss to explain the showstopping performance of a black American, Jesse Owens *(right).*

After winning the 100-meter dash—the first of four gold medals he would claim—Owens outdueled German champion Lutz Long in the broad jump, setting an Olympic record on his final leap. After the contest, Owens and Long walked arm in arm about the stadium to the crowd's cheers—proof that the Olympic ideal still flickered.

Friendly rivals, Lutz Long of Germany and Jesse Owens of the United States chat on the stadium turf. Long pressed Owens to the limit in the broad jump and finished second.

Silver medalist Helene Mayer *(above)* offers the Nazi salute. Mayer, who was half-Jewish, was named to the Olympic squad only after pressure from abroad.

Theodor Lewald *(below)*, who was president of the German Olympic Committee until he was ousted in 1933, speaks at the games' opening ceremony.

Germany's Harvest of Gold

If the Berlin Olympics failed to sustain Hitler's notion that Aryans were inherently superior, they nevertheless encouraged a Nazi regime that was putting extraordinary emphasis on physical conditioning. By the time the games came to an end, German athletes had captured thirty-three gold medals, and eighty-nine in all, to lead in both categories. The runner-up United States collected a total of fifty-six medals, twenty-four of them gold.

Germany's champions were a diverse lot, ranging from Karl Hein *(right),* a carpenter who won the hammer throw, to the elite cavalrymen who swept the gold in all of the individual and team equestrian events *(below).* Whatever their specialties, the Reich's medalists benefited from a training program of radical intensity, designed not only to impress the world but to inspire millions of German youngsters who were preparing in schoolyards and campgrounds to compete for Hitler in a more hazardous arena.

Captain Ludwig Stubbendorf and his horse Nurmi splash through a water hazard on the way to a gold medal in the rugged three-day equestrian event.

Germany's Karl Hein demonstrates the form that enabled him to break a twenty-four-year-old Olympic record in the hammer throw on his final fling.

882

Jugend dient dem Führer

THREE

"Things We Believed In, We Must Forget"

Few Germans dreamed of the wrenching changes that lay in store for their society on the eve of the Nazi revolution. To be sure, there were unmistakable signs of a deepening national crisis—political paralysis, widespread unemployment, pitched battles in the streets between rival extremist factions. Yet most Germans still had jobs to do, homes to keep, or schools to attend and adhered reflexively to their familiar routines. Indeed, for many young people, the narrow regularity of their lives in this time of diminishing prospects was more oppressive than any fear of what the future might hold.

To Horst Kruger, born in the middle-class Berlin suburb of Eichkamp in the aftermath of the Great War, the daily round in his household before Hitler seized power was numbingly predictable: "Get up at 6:30, wash, eat breakfast and put on a cheerful face, go to school, come home to dinner keeping warm in the oven; then homework upstairs, the window open, life beckoning, but back to the books; then my father's return around 4:30, a feeble hope that something would happen—that he might have brought something unusual from town. But nothing ever happened at our house; everything was normal, regulated, in order."

Kruger recalled with dismay his father's unshakable routine: "All his life he left home for the ministry at 8:23 a.m., traveling second class." The elder Kruger, the son of a manual laborer, had been wounded at Verdun and on his recovery in 1918 had found a civil-service job as a messenger. In time, he was made an administrator, "a breathtaking pinnacle," Horst wrote sarcastically, "that enjoined upon him eternal loyalty and submission to the state. His office was his world, and heaven was his wife. All his life, he came home at 4:21 p.m., always on the same train, always in the same second-class compartment."

A brown-shirted youngster matches the gaze of his Führer in a poster urging ten-year-olds to join the Hitler Youth. Each child who enlisted swore a solemn oath "to the savior of our country, Adolf Hitler. I am willing and ready to give up my life for him, so help me God."

Sundays were the worst for the young Kruger. His mother was a Catholic who had almost become a nun. His father, by contrast, "shared the rude kind of Berlin Protestantism that expresses its faith only in rabid and sneering anti-Catholicism." The elder Kruger never attended church; his wife professed a deep desire to go, but on most Sundays around 11 a.m.

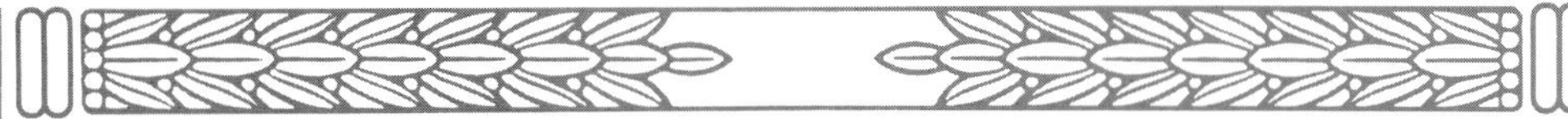

experienced sudden heart palpitations and took to the couch. And so, recalled Horst, "it mostly fell to me. I was the youngest. I couldn't defend myself, and so I was sent to church for the whole family." In deference to his mother's devotion, he worshiped as a Catholic, but he never regarded himself as such: "I wasn't Protestant either. I was more or less nothing, like most citizens of Eichkamp."

For years, the clockwork comings and goings of his father, the monotonous litanies of home, school, and church, proceeded undisturbed. Then came the first indication that something had shifted beneath the stolid foundation of this "narrow, vapid petite bourgeoisie." It was 1933, a cold night in January. His parents had tuned in a broadcast on the radio describing a parade in Berlin. "The radio announcer," Kruger recalled, "whose resonant tones were closer to singing and sobbing than reporting, was experiencing ineffable events; there seemed to be an indescribable exultation in the Reich capital's street of splendor." There was a new, young chancellor named Hitler. Sounds of masses marching and shouting erupted from the radio "and then again the sobbing voice, chanting something about Germany's reawakening."

Boys playing soldier march down a Hanover street in imitation of their Nazi elders during the celebration of Hitler's forty-fourth birthday on April 20, 1933.

In living rooms across Germany, the people listened on that winter night to what sounded to Kruger like "a Hallelujah Chorus of the redeemed." Reactions varied widely, of course, in a nation where peasant farmers living in something akin to medieval serfdom plowed fields next-door to modern aircraft factories; where adoring monarchists doted on gossip about their favorite Hohenzollern nobles at the same time their neighbors expounded

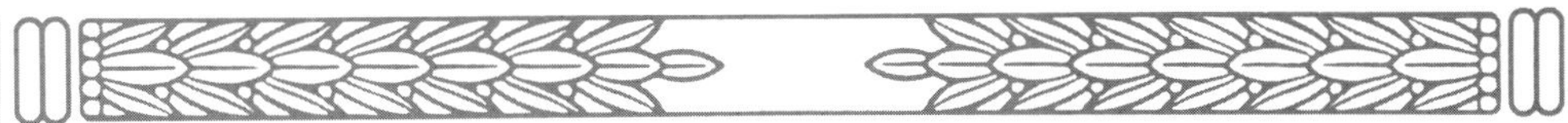

on the theories of Marx; where wives cherished the memory of husbands who had died in the last war while their hotheaded young sons dreamed of glory in the one to come.

At first, many uninvolved families such as the Krugers doubted that anyone could have much of an impact on the country's misfortunes. Then as the first months of Nazi power passed, wrote Kruger, "the skeptics relaxed." Horst, who had learned young that "a decent German is always unpolitical," was given a Nazi pennant for his bicycle; his mother had bought it from a Jewish merchant. And on a summer evening in 1933, he found his parents in their den, reading from a book titled *Mein Kampf.* "They read anxiously and expectantly," he recalled. "Their eyes were large and astonished, like those of children."

More compelling than Hitler's words were the ceremonies that sanctified his new regime. On holidays, the sleepy streets of Eichkamp took on the festive air of the Nazi shrine of Nuremberg, as the Krugers and their neighbors proclaimed their faith in the Reich with flags and anthems. Even charity drives became patriotic sacraments. Young Kruger recalled the Sunday when his family, as part of a nationwide campaign, made do with a one-dish meal and donated what they saved to the poor: "We all ate the lumpy barley soup in the conviction of having done something for the national community—an altogether new concept for Eichkamp."

The family's swift acceptance of the new regime was significant, because as Horst pointed out they belonged to that vast body of "innocuous Germans who were never Nazis, yet without whom the Nazis would never have been able to do their work." For the Krugers and those like them—who had found little inspiration in work, worship, or study—the sheer fervor of Hitler and his followers was bracing. "The citizens of Eichkamp were eager to give themselves over to intoxication and rapture."

The millions of Germans who yielded to that impulse and cheered Hitler's rise were in for a surprise. Beyond the rapture lay the reality of the new Nazi order—a sweeping social revolution that would impose rigid standards of behavior not only in schools, workplaces, and churches, but within the home. The citizens of the Third Reich would soon find themselves living in an eerie world of watchers and the watched. Children would be set against parents, wives against husbands, neighbor against neighbor. And inevitably, disillusionment would set in, but not before Hitler's functionaries had gained a virtual stranglehold on the institutions of daily life.

No single target of nazification took higher priority than Germany's young people. In the view of Nazi party theorists, the nation's adults had been exposed to too many dangerous ideas over the years and had become

accustomed to thinking and acting independently. The country's children, however, were malleable; they could be separated from the old ideas and inculcated with the Führer's new precepts. "The German youth of the future," proclaimed Hitler, "must be slim and slender, swift like the greyhound, tough like leather, and hard like Krupp steel." It was no accident that none of these adjectives referred to mental capacity. Hitler himself had been a dull student, fond only of gymnastics and drawing; the lessons he valued most were those that he had learned as a soldier, and his prescription for education reflected his bias: "I will have no intellectual training. Knowledge is ruin to my young men. A violently active, dominating, brutal youth—that is what I am after."

Before 1933, Germany's educational system, extending from kindergarten to university, had been admired throughout the world for its comprehensiveness. Yet this system was a product of Germany's imperial past, and its instructors—poorly paid civil servants whose lot improved little in the Weimar era—were predominantly conservative and nationalistic. Some of them were openly anti-Semitic, and cautionary texts such as Hans Grimm's *People without Space*—which anticipated Hitler's call for lebensraum—figured prominently in the curricula. Once in power, the Nazis swiftly capitalized on this reactionary trend, winning the support of teachers even at the elementary level, where some Social Democrats had obtained posts in recent years. Indeed, the elementary teachers yielded to the Nazis so readily that a sly riddle began to circulate: "What is the shortest measurable unit of time? The time it takes for a grade-school teacher to change his political allegiance."

In the secondary schools, where some teachers had encouraged independent thinking, the Nazi takeover had an immediate and chilling effect. One of those to feel it was a seventeen-year-old student named Hiltgunt Zassenhaus. In late 1932, she had attended a speech by Hitler and summed up her reactions in a trenchant essay. "The loudness of his voice can silence you," she wrote, "but it cannot convince. Hitler is a psychotic." Her teacher gave the paper an *A*. On the day that Hitler became Reich chancellor, the same instructor called Zassenhaus to her office and returned the essay. "Take it and burn it!" she said haltingly. "The things we believed in until now, we must forget."

During the first few months of Nazi rule, school administrators sympathetic to the cause dismissed teachers who were Jewish, politically unreliable, or married women—a group that the Nazis hoped to confine to domestic tasks. This process had no legal basis and was tentative at first but soon accelerated. It became obvious that a teacher's job security would depend on loyalty to the party. Within a few years of Hitler's ascension, 97

German children pore over an anti-Semitic schoolbook, *The Poisonous Mushroom.* Like a companion volume titled *Trust No Fox (held by the girl at left),* it sought to instill hatred of Jews in the very young.

percent of Germany's instructors had joined the Nazi teachers' association.

Whether students in 1933 were impressed by the purging of their instructors or not, they were soon transfixed by more theatrical measures. Elementary students were called out to throw their colored caps into bonfires. The hats had branded the children with their academic standing; the fires celebrated the end of such distinctions. Soon pupils consigned their textbooks to similar fires or saw the volumes carted off to the pulp mills to be recycled into something more useful to the Reich. Slender pamphlets recounting the life of the Führer or other edifying tales replaced bulky expositions of history, literature, and the sciences. Even math problems were rephrased to encourage combative thoughts: "A modern bomber can carry 1,800 incendiaries. How long is the path along which it can distribute these bombs if it drops a bomb every second at a speed of 250 kilometers per hour? How far apart are the craters?"

Reflecting the regime's commitment to rearmament, the time allotted to physical training was more than doubled. Meanwhile, fewer and fewer hours were devoted to religious instruction, foreign history, and literature. Passing the once-dreaded examinations became a matter of regurgitating Nazi biological theories and myths about the country's recent history. Nazi educators' contempt for the truth was most apparent in the teachings on race. When students entered the first grade, they were given a primer whose cover bore an unpleasant caricature of a Jew and the imprecation

Primers in Hate

Made all the more grotesque by the gay colors in which they are rendered, the illustrations reproduced here are from the racist primer *Trust No Fox in the Green Meadow and No Jew on His Oath (left)*. Issued in 1936 by the hate-mongering publisher Julius Streicher, the book was advertised as a Christmas gift for grade-schoolers. Two years later, Streicher published *The Poisonous Mushroom*, an anthology of cautionary tales for the young about the danger of associating with Jews. Together, the two volumes sold in the hundreds of thousands.

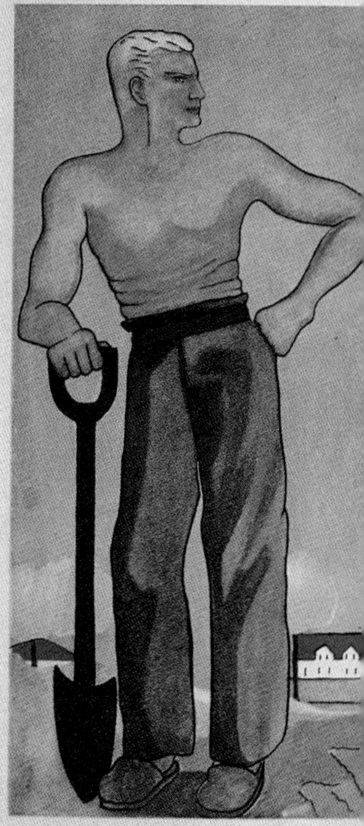

The introduction to *Trust No Fox* sets the book's tone by contrasting a blond Aryan "who can work and fight" with a repellently caricatured Jew, described as the "greatest scoundrel in the Reich." The text was printed in the penmanship style then taught in German schools, with key phrases emphasized in red.

"That's Streicher!" chirp young admirers of the anti-Semitic publisher and gauleiter of Franconia, who receives a bouquet of flowers given in appreciation for showing children "what it means to be Jewish and what it means to be German."

Aryan tots jeer as Jewish children and a Jewish teacher are expelled from school, where, according to the accompanying text, proper "discipline and order" can now be taught.

Dies ist der Jud, das sieht man gleich,
Der größte Schuft im ganzen Reich!
Er meint, daß er der Schönste sei
Und ist so häßlich doch dabei!

An Aryan boy cheerfully plays the accordian as Jews march into exile past a sign that reads ominously, "One-way street."

"Trust no Jew on his oath!" In biology, students were taught that their own species consisted of three classifications: Nordics, subhumans such as Slavs, and the antihuman Jews.

Few Jews were exposed to these rantings in class, because Jewish students were being routed from the public schools. In April 1933, the Decree against the Overcrowding of German Schools set an admissions quota of 1.5 percent for non-Aryans. And hostile students and teachers drove away many of those who made the quota, leaving it to Jewish communities to educate their own. Some youths of full or mixed Jewish ancestry stayed on, only to be steeped in doctrines that were an affront to their very identity. Lotte Paepcke, a Jewish woman married to a Christian, decided to conceal her heritage from her eight-year-old son. One evening, she recalled, the boy returned from school to inform his parents that "the Führer never slept, so great was his concern for the people, and that Jews should be struck whenever one comes across them." His mother was speechless: "The blood rushed to my head, I was so appalled by the enormity of the moment and my inability to say, 'Look, here's a Jew sitting right in front of you—your own mother!' But the boy was still so childish and so naive and so inclined to blurt out everything he knew that we didn't dare enlighten him."

Not content with pervasive control of the school system, Hitler's bureaucrats intruded even further into the lives of students, teachers, and parents through the Nazi youth movement. In 1933, more than five million German youngsters belonged to various organizations that stressed sports, hiking, and camping and encouraged young people to criticize the conventions of their parents' generation and think of themselves as the hope of the future. "Youth must be led by youth" was a slogan used frequently. In January 1933, the Hitler Youth, with only 55,000 members, was one of the smaller of these groups.

That situation was soon remedied. In the summer of 1933, Hitler appointed Baldur von Schirach, the twenty-six-year-old son of a noble German family, youth leader of the German Reich. A plump and effeminate figure, Schirach was a paradoxical young man. He was an aristocrat who despised his own class, a student organizer who had been expelled from his fraternity and never graduated from a university, and a writer of maudlin verses who displayed a steely resolve to destroy all opposition. Under his leadership, the Hitler Youth was to become the largest organization for young people ever seen in the Western world.

With the help of some powerful allies, Schirach's group soon dispensed with the competition. In June 1933, the Whitsunday camp of the Greater German League, a large youth association that had been set up by con-

Amid memorial wreaths and fuming torches, the Reich youth leader, Baldur von Schirach, delivers a radio address from the grave site of Herbert Norkus, a fifteen-year-old member of the Hitler Youth. Norkus was stabbed to death in January of 1932 while posting Nazi placards in a communist district of Berlin. His murder became a rallying point for the Hitler Youth.

Herbert Norkus
* 26·7·1916
† 24·1·1932

servative groups as an alternative to the Hitler Youth, was surrounded by police and SA men; the campers were sent home, and two weeks later the league disbanded. Elsewhere, brownshirted Hitler Youth did their own dirty work, raiding the offices of rival groups and turning the files over to authorities for action. Before the summer was out, the Führer simply incorporated most of the surviving associations into the Hitler Youth by decree. By year's end, membership had increased forty times to 2.3 million, or 30 percent of all Germans between ten and eighteen years of age.

In the beginning, membership in the Hitler Youth was supposedly voluntary, but the student who demurred encountered a combination of blandishments and pressure that only the hardiest could resist. One group of boys who clung to membership in the Catholic Youth Club were asked to submit an essay titled "Why Am I Not in the Hitler Youth?" The teacher who made the assignment left them little choice: "If you don't write the essay, I shall beat you until you can't sit down!" Asked why he frequently hit recalcitrant young Catholics but never young Nazis, the same teacher responded, "It goes against the grain to beat a boy wearing the brown shirt of honor."

Most boys required little prodding to wear that outfit. "What I liked about the Hitler Youth was the comradeship," recalled one individual who at the youngest-possible age enlisted in the German Jungvolk, the division for boys aged ten to fourteen. "I was full of enthusiasm. What boy isn't fired up by being presented with high ideals such as comradeship, loyalty, and honor?" Then, too, there were the snappy uniforms, the impressive parades, the solemn vows of loyalty to the Führer. It was heady stuff for a ten-year-old boy. To qualify for membership and receive his first dagger, he had to participate in war games and a day-and-a-half-long march, achieve a set of minimum standards on the playing field, and pass tests of his knowledge of Nazi arcana, including the words of the "Horst Wessel Song." But after months of meetings, encampments, parade-ground drill, small-arms practice, semaphore instruction, and indoctrination, his enthusiasm dimmed. Though awarded leadership rank, he found "the compulsion and the requirement of absolute obedience unpleasant."

Other boys who joined chafed at the discipline that was meted out by

Hitler Youth leaders little older than themselves. One recruit recalled the spectacle of "twelve-year-old horde leaders bawling out ten-year-old cubs and driving them all over the school playground and meadows. The slightest signs of recalcitrance, the slightest faults with our uniforms, the slightest lateness on parade were punished with extra drill. But there was method in the madness: From childhood onward, we were drilled in toughness and blind obedience."

Attracted by cheerful posters such as the one at left, members of the League of German Girls received physical and ideological indoctrination that ranged from tumbling, shown below, to memorizing names of Nazi martyrs.

The League of Young Girls (ages ten to fourteen) and the League of German Girls (ages fourteen to eighteen) —the girls' divisions of the Hitler Youth—were organized along different lines. The physical requirements were scaled down, and greater emphasis was placed on the mastery of domestic tasks, in keeping with Nazi doctrine on the subordinate, homemaking role of women. In order to polish such skills, a special organization was created for girls between seventeen and twenty-one years of age. Called Faith and Beauty, it emphasized a combination of domestic handiness and homespun feminine charm. Long braids and ankle-length gowns were de rigueur, and any girl who broke ranks and permed her hair risked having it shaved off.

In addition to their Hitler Youth activities, students who had completed their elementary education were required to help with the harvest each year. Some spent an entire year at an agricultural camp, working in the morning and receiving lessons in National Socialist ideology in the afternoon. For a nine-month stretch, the youngsters at these camps were allowed no vacations, parental visits, or religious services. The Nazis touted the experience as an opportunity

A Uniform Code for the Young

"Everyone who is of German blood belongs to our group," asserted Reich Youth Leader Baldur von Schirach, and all "wear the garb of the community of comrades, the brown shirt of the Hitler Youth." The brown shirt had been authorized for youthful Nazis as early as 1926. But in those days of rampant street violence, children under the age of fourteen were restricted from wearing a swastika with it, lest they be mistaken for Storm Troopers.

In 1933, several standardized Hitler Youth uniforms were offered for sale through strictly licensed "brown shops," the Nazi party's uniform stores. A diamond-backed swastika device was worn by all members except the Jungvolk, or Young People, aged ten to fourteen, who wore an S-shaped runic device on their sleeve.

Members of the League of German Girls were at first issued a simple brown costume called a gym slip. Hitler objected: "We don't want our girls dressed so that no man will give them a second look!" To resolve the Führer's complaint, a group of Berlin designers created a stylish new costume in 1936.

During the winter, German girls wore a climbing jacket *(above, right)* with the Hitler Youth patch on its left sleeve. A young women's unit that specialized in first aid carried the pennant.

The brown shirt and khaki cap above, worn with shorts and neckerchief, were summer dress for Hitler Youth. In 1934, the blue ski suit and cap at right were introduced as a winter uniform. The trumpet above bears the S-rune of the German Jungvolk.

for urban youth to commune with the rural folk and shake off the supposedly debilitating effects of book learning. "The true, great, practical school," proclaimed the Prussian minister of education, was to be found not in the classroom but "in the labor camp, for here instruction and words cease and action begins."

Far from promoting universal health and happiness, the rigorous activities sponsored by the Nazis caused an increase in physical and psychological ailments among the young. Complaints ranged from anxiety brought on by ceaseless bullying to disorders of the feet caused by carrying burdens that were too heavy on marches that were too long. A child's participation in the Hitler Youth could create friction at home. Some parents who were opposed to the regime tried to discourage their youngsters from joining the organization, to little avail. A secret report by the Social Democratic underground noted ruefully that German parents "cannot forbid the child to do what all children are doing, cannot refuse him the uniform that the others have." Nor could dissident parents safely ignore their youngsters' demands that they, too, "become good Nazis, that they give up Marxism, reaction, and dealings with Jews." Political conflicts aside, parents sometimes had trouble keeping their brown-shirted sons and daughters in line. One ten-year-old convert, on being instructed to play with a neighbor girl of similar age, responded curtly, "It's out of the question. I'm in uniform."

The most obvious side effect of the Nazi youth movement, however, was the precipitate decline in the quality of education. Students frequently missed classes to take part in Hitler Youth outings, and teachers could do little about it. In 1937, members of a Bavarian chapter of the Nazi teachers' association complained officially: "There is widespread lack of any keenness or commitment. Many pupils believe they can simply drift through for eight years." The report criticized Hitler Youth leaders in particular for displaying "unmannerly behavior and laziness. School discipline has declined to an alarming extent."

Not surprisingly, the products of the Nazi school system were held in generally low esteem. Graduates who sought, for example, to join what had been one of the best-trained and best-educated officer corps in the world were found by one authority to display an "inconceivable lack of elementary knowledge." Many young people began to question the value of obtaining the once-prestigious *Abitur,* the graduation certificate needed to enter a university. By the late 1930s, seventeen of twenty students were dropping out of school to work as craft apprentices or industrial trainees.

The Nazi approach to educational reform—typically grandiose in its designs, ruthless in its tactics, and muddled in its execution—had an

University students in SA uniforms parade across a bridge in Heidelberg. The disruptive agendas of the Nazi-run German Student Association and the SA —which conducted paramilitary training on campuses—led many undergraduates to turn their backs on academic pursuits. As one student leader said, "We have no respect for the clever monks in their quiet cells."

equally disruptive effect on the universities. Like the nation's public schools, they were purged in 1933. Fifteen percent of the nation's university teachers were fired because they were Jewish or deemed politically unreliable. In addition, many independent-minded scholars and researchers saw the import of the Nazi designs and left the country. The losses in some sensitive scientific areas were so serious that Nazi Germany would never recover from them. David Hilbert, a mathematician at the University of Göttingen, was asked by Hitler's minister of education, Bernhard Rust, whether his department had suffered as a result of the dismissal of Jews. "Suffered?" Hilbert replied. "No, it hasn't suffered, Herr Minister. It just doesn't exist any more."

University students had their equivalent of the Hitler Youth—the German Student Association. It, too, was commanded by Schirach, who had begun agitating for the Nazis on campuses as early as 1926. By January 1933, his association already claimed half of the country's college students as members. They participated in the celebratory march through Berlin and in May

ceremonially burned 20,000 books considered to threaten the Nazi state. Membership was soon made mandatory, and students were required to put aside their texts and spend two months in an SA camp and four months in a labor camp before they graduated. These provisions conveniently reduced overcrowding on the campuses but also lowered educational standards. Entering freshmen who had spent a few years in the Nazi school system were unprepared for even the watered-down requirements of the revised university curricula, and most students spent their first year in remedial classes. With the continual round of marches, rallies, and camps required of them, they never had time to catch up, and desperate professors were forced to ease their requirements drastically in order to graduate sufficient numbers.

To make matters worse for Nazi educators, the initial wave of enthusiasm for their cause on campuses gave way to apathy. Attendance at party meetings and rallies lagged. At the University of Cologne in 1935, the Nazis organized a celebration on May Day—an official holiday in the Third Reich. Of the university's 3,000 students, only 200 attended the event. Shocked, student leaders called a mandatory assembly of the student body to boost morale, but one of the rally's organizers admitted that this forced show of school spirit was "pure chicanery."

Such incidents on the campuses underscored a problem that plagued the entire Nazi youth movement—festering dissatisfaction with the regime's coercive ways. By the late 1930s, a few rebels began to defy authority openly. Working-class youngsters formed gangs that roamed the streets and brawled with Hitler Youth detachments, while middle-class malcontents gathered at clubs in the cities to flaunt their long hair and dance to the swing music that Nazi propagandists denounced as degenerate. A Hitler Youth informant reported on a Hamburg swing conclave: "At the entrance to the hall stood a notice on which the words 'Swing prohibited' had been altered to 'Swing requested.' The participants accompanied the dances and songs, without exception, by singing the English words. Indeed, throughout the evening they attempted to speak only English; at some tables, even French. The band played wilder and wilder items; none of the players was sitting down any longer; they all 'jitterbugged' on the stage like wild creatures. Several boys could be observed dancing together, always with two cigarettes in the mouth, one in each corner."

Nazi officials sensed from the start that the public schools and universities, where some diversity of opinion was inevitable, might not be the best training grounds for the future leaders of the Third Reich. The new order would need officers and administrators who were both competent and

uncontaminated by subversive thoughts. Those qualities could best be inculcated in special academies. In the chaotic fashion typical of the regime, several agencies—the Reich Ministry of Education, Nazi party, Hitler Youth, SA, and SS—vied for the honor of filling the bill. The result was two rival systems of elite schools.

In 1933, the SA, SS, and Education Ministry reached an uneasy agreement to set up boarding schools for boys called National Political Education Institutions (Napolas). They were intended to succeed the Prussian cadet academies and train leaders for both military and civil service. But the SS soon elbowed its way into control and focused the Napolas' efforts on producing officer candidates for the expanding armed branch of Heinrich Himmler's organization.

Each Napola—there were twenty-one by 1938—received about 400 applications a year from ten-year-olds. After the sons of leading party officials, civil servants, and army officers were allotted their places, the rest of the applicants were screened and about 100 selected for the tough entrance examinations. These lasted several days—academic tests in the morning, physical-training competitions in the afternoon, and military exercises at night. Two-thirds of the candidates failed. The survivors left their homes for eight years of military formations, political indoctrination, and snippets of rudimentary education. Graduates apparently satisfied the requirements of the SS for officer candidates, but according to the SS general who supervised the Napolas, their academic standards were "below those of the average grammar school."

In 1937, the Nazi party inaugurated a program to train its own leaders in Adolf Hitler Schools. The chief criteria for selection were a suitably Aryan appearance and a good record during the first two years of membership in the Hitler Youth. Promising twelve-year-olds who passed an inspection of their racial heritage and performed satisfactorily at a two-week evaluation camp were inducted into an Adolf Hitler School regardless of their parents' wishes. There the boys encountered five periods of physical training a day and only one and a half of academic study. The atmosphere in the classroom was casual, but life in the barracks and on the parade ground was rigidly disciplined. Ten leadership schools were eventually established. Their graduates had learned the approved way to make a bed and clean a rifle, but their ignorance of other matters made it difficult for them to command much respect.

Still hoping to nurture an elite, the Nazi party in the late 1930s created four finishing schools for outstanding graduates of the Adolf Hitler Schools and other promising young Nazis. These institutions, called Castles of the Order, attempted to re-create a medieval order of chivalry. They were in fact

castles located in remote, scenic locations, each requiring a staff of 500 faculty members and uniformed servants to minister to 1,000 students. The schools featured ornate architecture—including the world's largest gymnasium at one and a marble dining hall seating 1,500 at another—and exotic programs of physical training to complement the political indoctrination. Students traveled from one castle to another through the year and mastered sailing, gliding, skiing, mountain climbing, and horseback riding—the last activity intended, in the words of Nazi party organizer Robert Ley, to give the young men "the feeling of being able to dominate a living creature entirely."

It was no oversight that the special Nazi academies had no slots for girls. At their first general meeting in 1921, the National Socialists had resolved, "A woman can never be accepted into the leadership of the party." Hitler and his partisans envisioned a Reich where men would be honored as warriors and providers and women would serve mainly as breeders and nurturers. The Nazis denounced the movement toward equality of the sexes under the Weimar Republic, which accorded women the vote and a small but increasing role in a paternalistic society. By the end of the 1920s, Germany had more women in its parliament than any other western country. In 1933, the employment rate for women in Germany was four times that in the United States.

Once in power, the National Socialists sought to reverse this trend by driving married women from the workplace and blocking avenues of advancement for all women. Government directives banned married women from the civil service, drastically limited the number of female students admitted to the universities, and barred women from serving as judges, public prosecutors, or jury members. Explaining the latter policy, one newspaper reported that women "cannot think logically or reason objectively, since they are ruled only by emotion."

Women continued to play an important part in the economy, however. As the depression eased in the mid-1930s and men returned to work in droves, the proportion of women in the labor force declined slightly, from about one in three to roughly one in four. But by 1937, Germany's rearmament program had helped create a labor shortage, and Nazi officials found themselves in the contradictory position of having to encourage women to work. Increasingly, women opted for better-paying jobs in the larger towns, leaving behind servant's work and the hard life on the farm. The trend became so pronounced the government decreed in 1938 that women taking certain desirable jobs first had to spend a "duty year" working as farm laborers or domestics.

A printed slogan, "The German woman does not smoke," hangs conspicuously in a restaurant in Ulm. The Nazi campaign against smoking by women was sometimes enforced by Storm Troopers, who would declare, "The Führer disapproves!" and then snatch the cigarette from a woman's mouth.

If the regime failed to constrict the economic role of women, it was more successful at altering their appearance and habits. The party regarded such things as fashionable clothing, makeup, and work pants on women as evidence of Weimar decadence. Maintaining a slim figure and smoking cigarettes were branded as detrimental to fertility and thus un-German. The official image of the ideal woman was of a plump, broad-hipped, fresh-faced, primly gowned, unadorned peasant girl with blond hair pulled into a bun or coiled braid. Those who deliberately defied this stereotype might be disciplined by their professional associations, fired from their

jobs, or publicly denounced as "trouser-wenches with Indian warpaint." Those who conformed improved their chances of attracting or holding a mate in a society where war casualties had resulted in a significant surplus of women. A marriage advertisement in 1935 spelled out the ideal sought by ambitious men of the day: "Fifty-two-year-old, pure Aryan physician, fighter at Tannenberg, wishing to settle down, desires male offspring through civil marriage with young, healthy virgin of pure Aryan stock, undemanding, suited to heavy work and thrifty, with flat heels, without earrings, if possible without money."

German women offered little resistance to the Nazi crusade against the trappings of liberation. Most submitted to the new vogue. ("I was struck by the ugliness of German women," an American reporter wrote in the 1930s. "They dress worse than English women used to.") Under pressure from the party, millions flocked to the German Women's League, which offered enlightenment on such subjects as cooking leftovers, making clothes with good German cloth, and raising babies. Although it tolerated a small but vocal feminist faction, the league firmly encouraged women to embrace their second-class role. Gertrud Scholtz-Klink, the *Reichsfrauenführerin*, or Reich women's leader, proclaimed, "Even though our weapon is only the soup ladle, its impact should be as great as that of other weapons." Scholtz-Klink herself, despite the imposing title she possessed, had little impact on Nazi policymakers, who excluded her from meetings at which issues affecting women were discussed.

While a woman's work was often slighted in the Third Reich, her ability to bear children was celebrated to the point of adulation. Increasing the population of Germany was one of the main concerns of Hitler's regime, intent as it was on building and maintaining a vast army. Between 1900 and 1933, the German birthrate had declined more than 50 percent because of war, economic uncertainty, and a growing awareness of the methods of contraception. The National Socialists moved on several fronts to encourage the formation and enlargement of families, referred to as "germ cells of the nation." The most effective measures were financial—marriage loans, child bonuses, and family allowances. Newlyweds whose racial, mental, and physical qualifications were judged acceptable were offered interest-free loans of up to 1,000 reichsmarks, provided that the wife did not work. Payments were set at one percent a month, a relatively light burden for a family that was earning the average industrial wage of 150 reichsmarks per month. For every child born to the union, one-fourth of the loan was forgiven. In 1937, the restriction on female employment was dropped, but if the wife worked, the loan payments were tripled. Those families with more than four children under the age of sixteen could take advantage of

additional incentives. There were one-time bonuses of up to 100 reichsmarks given for each child. And every month the family would receive an allowance: 10 marks each for the third and fourth children, and 20 marks for each additional child.

German couples responded as hoped to these enticements. The birthrate jumped from 14.7 per thousand people in 1933 to 18 per thousand by the end of 1934 and to 20.4 by 1939. During the first six years of the Reich, 1.1 million marriage loans were made; 980,000 were at least partially forgiven by births. The Nazis applied to this project not only large sums of money but the full force of their vaunted propaganda apparatus. The act of giving birth was extolled as "donating a child to the Führer." The word *family* became a title of honor, restricted to those couples who had contributed at least four children. Women who made further "donations" were awarded a bronze Mother's Cross for the fifth delivery, a silver cross for the sixth, and a gold one for the seventh.

Young women capering on the grounds of a school for homemakers exemplify the hearty, rustic look promoted by the regime—simple folk dresses, plaited or pulled-back hair, and full figures suggestive of fertility. Hitler, however, favored women of an "elegant, slim figure."

In addition to encouraging approved behavior, the government harshly

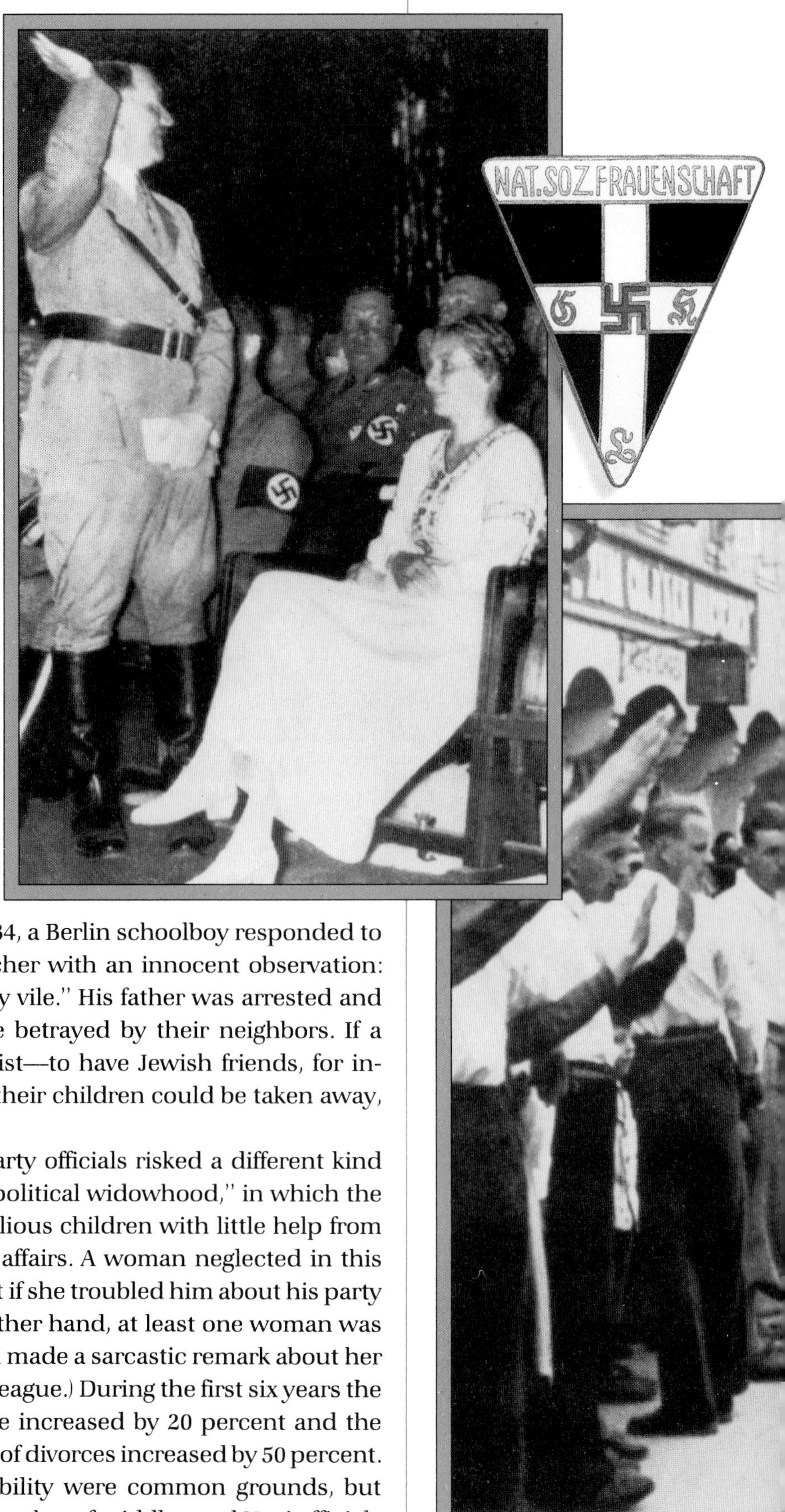

penalized opposition. Abortions were branded "acts of sabotage," and doctors convicted of performing them received lengthy jail sentences. The advertisement of contraceptives was banned, although their manufacture and sale remained legal. Since the Nazi regime was interested in increasing the population of only healthy Germans, people with defects that were thought to be inheritable were forcibly sterilized.

For all the official attention accorded it, the German family became an increasingly troubled unit. Militant children absorbed in their own fanatical organizations had little reason to afford their parents attention, let alone respect, and were encouraged to denounce to the authorities elders who made misstatements. Sometimes children informed on their mothers and fathers unwittingly. In 1934, a Berlin schoolboy responded to the anti-Semitic statements of his teacher with an innocent observation: "My daddy says Jews are not damnably vile." His father was arrested and tortured. In other cases, parents were betrayed by their neighbors. If a couple was judged to be nonconformist—to have Jewish friends, for instance, or to be Jehovah's Witnesses—their children could be taken away, to be raised by a more reliable family.

Women who married well-placed party officials risked a different kind of punishment—a fate referred to as "political widowhood," in which the wife struggled to raise a brood of rebellious children with little help from a husband enmeshed in bureaucratic affairs. A woman neglected in this way could not divorce her husband, but if she troubled him about his party duties, he could divorce her. (On the other hand, at least one woman was granted a divorce because her husband made a sarcastic remark about her membership in the German Women's League.) During the first six years the Nazis were in power, the marriage rate increased by 20 percent and the birthrate by 45 percent, but the number of divorces increased by 50 percent. Childlessness and political incompatibility were common grounds, but those seeking divorce also included a number of middle-aged Nazi officials

Reich Women's Leader Gertrud Scholtz-Klink *(below)* acknowledges Nazi salutes on a 1938 visit to Austria. Although Scholtz-Klink often appeared at Hitler's side *(far left)*, she was largely a figurehead who lent a wholesome air to the regime and urged those in her women's league to do the same. The league's pin *(near left)* bore the initials of the words *faith, hope,* and *charity,* but not all of the league's activities were benevolent; some of its members became guards at an early prison camp for women.

ridding themselves of middle-aged wives in favor of younger and more alluring companions. Heinrich Himmler, with encouragement from Hitler, dreamed of fostering a special order of biologically and politically pure young women who would serve as new mates for Nazi leaders, supplanting those "good, trusty housewives who were entirely in place during the time of struggle but no longer suit their husbands today."

At all levels of society, the preoccupation with breeding Aryans lessened the constraints against premarital sex and illegitimate birth. Both Himmler's SS and the Nazi party established comfortable nursing homes for the married and unwed mates of their members. And large political gatherings provided unmarried youngsters with golden opportunities to donate a child to the Führer. The Nuremberg rally of 1936 left 900 girls between the ages of fifteen and eighteen pregnant.

Increasingly, weddings took on a secular character, with religious pledges supplemented or replaced by solemn vows to Führer and country. As a girls' leader in the Hitler Youth recalled, the services reflected "the idea that the marriage was concluded as a duty to the nation. The religious content of these ceremonies was very general; indeed, one must call it muddled." Nor was this an isolated phenomenon. Under the Nazis, the very cornerstones of faith in Germany were being undermined.

Germany in 1933 could not have been characterized as a deeply religious country. The attitude of the Kruger family, with its designated churchgoer, was probably typical. Nevertheless, in the homeland of Martin Luther, the churches remained havens for millions who looked on God as the ultimate authority, an allegiance that Hitler found abhorrent.

Nominally, the country was two-thirds Protestant and one-third Catholic. The

Catholic church, strongest in Bavaria, was politically powerful because of its dominance of the Center party, which during most of the Weimar era had been part of the governing coalition in the Reichstag. The Protestants were less effective than their numbers would indicate because their religious organization was decentralized and their political influence divided among several parties, but they had been moving toward greater cohesion.

From the beginning, the Nazi party had paid lip service to religious values, endorsing what it called a positive Christianity. What positive Christianity entailed, aside from opposition to Jews and Marxists, the Nazis never explained. Before taking power, Hitler studiously avoided conflict with the churches. Indeed, by supporting their independence and their proper role in the affairs of state, by opposing godless communism and

A party official's wife *(below)* shows off the family's seventh child, whose birth earned the woman a gold Mother's Cross *(right)*. The Nazis encouraged couples either to procreate or to get a divorce.

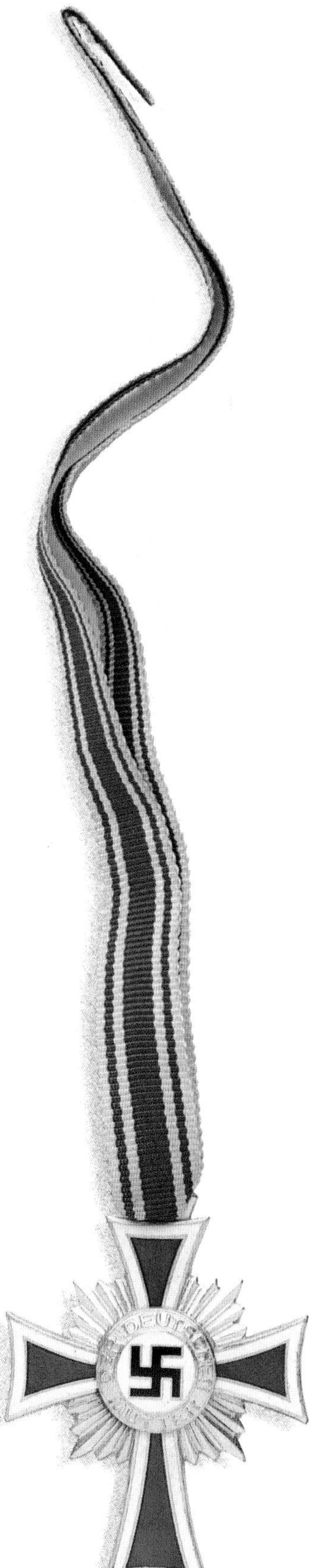

espousing the moral regeneration of Germany, he appealed to thousands of individual Christians. "I need the Catholics of Bavaria just as I need the Protestants of Prussia," he avowed.

Hitler was raised a Catholic but harbored little affection for the church of Rome. Privately, he voiced contempt for "hypocritical priests" and their "satanic superstition," and his Nazi deputies sparred with the representatives of the Catholic Center party in the Reichstag. Still, he regarded the power of the Vatican with mingled admiration and fear, and he hoped to avoid a direct confrontation with Rome.

Hitler's relations with the Protestant churches were easier. The dominant Protestant group—the Lutherans—were fond of quoting St. Paul's admonition, "The powers that be are ordained of God." They were led by pastors who were strongly paternalistic and patriotic and often suspicious of democratic reforms. In the waning years of the Weimar Republic, the Lutheran clergy found much to like in Hitler's doctrine of a new, powerful Germany, and some saw his program of positive Christianity as a godsend.

Sensing an opening, the Nazis in 1931 took an active role in Protestant affairs. They helped organize the so-called Faith Movement of German Christians, which like the Nazi youth and trade organizations set out to subvert the very ideals it purported to cherish. Led by the Reverend Joachim Hossenfelder, who became adviser to the Nazis on church affairs, the German Christians infiltrated all the major Protestant churches, where they advocated ultranationalism and anti-Semitism and called the faithful to political combat with Marxists and Catholics. Hossenfelder described his organization as the "SA of Jesus Christ."

Hitler's growing influence among the Protestants worried leaders of the Catholic minority, who feared persecution if they continued to oppose the Nazis. A few months after Hitler had been named chancellor, he appealed to the Catholic deputies of the Center and Bavarian People's parties to ratify the Enabling Act that would grant him absolute powers. Against the wishes of the ecclesiastical hierarchy, the Catholics voted with the Nazis and the conservatives to end democracy and launch the Third Reich.

Once the die had been cast, most Catholic and Protestant clergies hailed their new dictator. As an American observer noted: "They have confidence in him. They feel the need for a strong hand upon the nation." In public, Hitler reciprocated the warm feelings. "The national government sees in both Christian denominations the most important factor for the maintenance of our society," he told the docile new Reichstag. "The rights of the churches will not be diminished." Meanwhile, he revealed his true feelings in private, explaining to intimates that he would tolerate the churches temporarily for political reasons. "But," he added, "that won't stop me from

German Vice Chancellor Franz von Papen *(far left)* appears in Rome with Cardinal Eugenio Pacelli *(center)* on July 20, 1933, to sign the Vatican's concordat with Hitler. The Führer agreed to tolerate Catholic organizations but declared that German Catholics were expected to "put themselves without reservation at the service of the new National Socialist state."

stamping out Christianity in Germany, root and branch. One is either a Christian or a German. One can't be both!"

Within a week of Hitler's conciliatory Reichstag speech, the Catholic bishops of Germany announced that their "previous general warnings and prohibitions" opposing the Nazi movement "need no longer be considered necessary." A delighted Hitler seized on the opportunity to silence his Catholic critics for good. A few days later, Vice Chancellor Franz von Papen—a former leader of the Center party—arrived in the Vatican to negotiate a general treaty, or concordat, with Cardinal Eugenio Pacelli, the Vatican's secretary of state and the future pope, Pius XII. The Vatican wanted to protect its German clerics from persecution and forestall the establishment of Protestantism as the state religion, an apparent aim of the German Christian movement. Hitler wanted the Vatican to prohibit its clergy and its affiliated organizations from taking part in German politics. Agreement was quickly reached.

Meanwhile, the Lutheran church moved closer to Hitler—and to destruction. Leaders reorganized the twenty-eight provincial churches into one Reich Church under a single bishop, the better to assist the rebirth of Germany. Hitler approved so long as the bishop was a Nazi. As his nominee he plucked from obscurity a fifty-year-old military chaplain named Ludwig Müller. But the Lutherans, taking seriously the prospect of sharing power, selected their own man. Hitler expressed his "extreme regrets" at the development. The Prussian government took over the larger provincial Lutheran churches and fired their officers, replacing them with German Christian zealots who called themselves trustees of Jesus Christ. "For the first time," exulted a German Christian pastor, "a German in a brown shirt enters the church consistory." Buoyed by the turn of events, Müller de-

clared himself Reich bishop-elect and hastily prepared a new church constitution to legitimize his claim.

On July 14, 1933, Hitler had his cabinet approve the proposed treaty with the Vatican and the constitution for the Reich Church. Nine days later, German Christians won control of that body in a special church election. On August 1, an appalled Swedish journalist watched 200 German Christian clergymen convene a local synod "in brown uniforms, riding boots, body and shoulder straps, with all sorts of swastikas, badges of rank, and medals." The synod was brought to a close, he noted, with a rendition of "the repulsive 'Horst Wessel Song.' The whole thing could only be described as religious barbarism."

Catholic leaders entered into their new partnership with less ostentation but equal enthusiasm. Priests adorned their churches with swastikas, sang the "Horst Wessel Song" during mass, and praised Hitler from the pulpit. The Catholic Trade Union and Teachers' Federation obligingly disbanded. And even though Catholic youth groups stubbornly maintained their identity, Catholic university students pledged their loyalty to the Führer and learned to execute the stiff Nazi salute.

Some clerics of both faiths were revolted by these developments. Traditionalists among the Lutherans detected a note of blasphemy in the sermons of Bishop Müller's subalterns, one of whom proclaimed, "Christ has come to us through Adolf Hitler." In the fall of 1933, resistance to Nazi interference in Lutheran affairs crystallized around the imposing figure of Martin Niemöller, an influential pastor in Berlin. Niemöller, who had served as a U-boat commander during the war, sympathized with Hitler's call for national revival

A member of the pro-Nazi German Christian movement *(left)* and a rival from the Young Reformers hand out campaign literature during elections for the governing board of the new Protestant Reich Church in July 1933. Boosted by an election-eve radio address by Hitler, the German Christians prevailed.

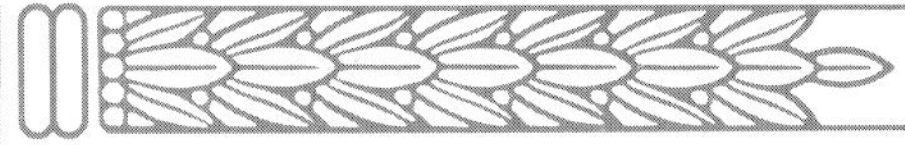

Women in traditional dress join Nazis at the investiture of Ludwig Müller *(behind lectern)* as Reich Church bishop. The Berlin rite followed his election in September 1933 at a synod dominated by the German Christians.

but balked when the Nazis tried to insert an article banning non-Aryan pastors into the Lutherans' cherished confession of faith. Niemöller circulated a letter calling on his colleagues to return to Holy Scripture and the Confessions of the Reformation. Two thousand clergymen soon joined his Pastors' Emergency League to resist the nazification of their church.

Niemöller's supporters were outraged in November when Reich Bishop Müller gathered with 20,000 of his supporters in Berlin to applaud the concept of "one mighty, new, all-embracing German people's church." The assembled were told by one speaker that the Old Testament of the Bible, "with its Jewish morality of rewards and its stories of cattle dealers and concubines," would be discarded, and that the New Testament would be cleansed of the ideas of the "Rabbi Paul." The remarks drove more members of the clergy into Niemöller's camp; by January of 1934, his league had approximately 7,000 members.

Shaken by the revolt, the regime brought its growing police powers to bear. Gestapo agents encouraged churchgoers to denounce dissident pastors, who were then barred from the pulpit. On January 24, one offending Berlin minister was dragged from his bed by five young toughs and beaten. The next day, Hitler exercised his own brand of intimidation. He called Niemöller and eleven other Lutheran leaders to his office and accused Niemöller of disloyalty to the state on the basis of remarks he had made in a taped telephone conversation. Niemöller firmly denied the charge, but his eleven colleagues hastily dissociated themselves from the Pastors' Emergency League. As Hitler recalled with satisfaction later, they "were so shaken with terror that they literally collapsed."

That night, the Gestapo raided Niemöller's home. A few days later, a bomb exploded in his hallway. He was forced to take a leave of absence, and his less well known associates were packed off to concentration camps. Niemöller continued his resistance until 1937, when he, too, was sent to a camp, a few days after delivering a defiant sermon: "No more are we ready to keep silent at man's behest when God commands us to speak."

Germany's Catholics, meanwhile, were learning for themselves what Hitler's pledge to respect religious traditions was worth. Not even an ironclad contract with the Nazi state could save the Catholic church from the brutal attentions of Nazi thugs. Early in 1934, the Nazis unleashed bands of Hitler Youth to bully Catholic youth groups into submission. The SS raided the other remaining Catholic organizations and forcibly disbanded them, confiscating their property. Undaunted, a few prominent German Catholics bravely protested Nazi policies that violated Church teachings. Bishop Clemens August Galen of Münster, for one, issued a pastoral letter in 1934 criticizing the forced-sterilization program. But most

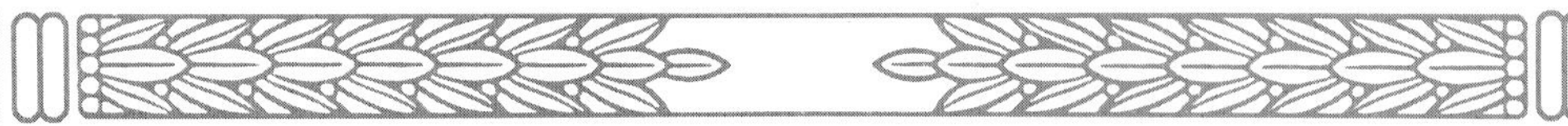

Catholics in positions of authority went along with the regime and prayed quietly that conditions would improve.

That hope persisted until June 30, 1934, when Hitler authorized the infamous Blood Purge, which was aimed ostensibly at recalcitrant SA leaders. On the long list of enemies abducted and shot, however, were several outspoken Catholic activists and writers. In light of these murders, there could no longer be any doubt about Hitler's determination to silence Christians of conscience, whatever their denomination. The Vatican was mute, while a leading Protestant bishop sent Hitler a telegram expressing "warmest thanks for firm rescue operation, along with best wishes and renewed promises of unalterable loyalty."

With the established churches effectively neutralized, the Nazis attempted to foster their own religion by replacing Christian rituals with secular ones that glorified the regime. The party issued guidelines for Nazi ceremonies "of a liturgical character, which shall be valid for centuries." These services began with a poetic proclamation, followed by a hazy confession of faith and a hymn of duty. They ended with a salute to the Führer and the singing of the national anthem and the "Horst Wessel Song." Children were taught to pray before meals, "Führer, my Führer, bequeathed to me by the Lord, protect and preserve me as long as I live."

To wean people from the Christian calendar, the Nazis promoted a busy cycle of festivals that celebrated pagan and political turning points: the anniversary of the seizure of power on January 30; Hitler's birthday on April 20; May Day; the summer solstice on June 21; the Nuremberg rally in September; a harvest festival in October; the anniversary of the Munich Putsch on November 9; and Yuletide, a replacement for Christmas, on the winter solstice, December 21. This new calendar was observed with particular zeal in Himmler's SS, which took the trend toward secular religion further by instituting its own rites for baptisms, weddings, and burials. A typical SS marriage ceremony took place by the light of torches, with chanted refrains from a Wagnerian opera, a reading from Norse

The Gestapo hounded Martin Niemöller for denouncing the Lutheran church's nazification. "God is giving Satan a free hand so that it may be seen what manner of men we are," he said.

Ringed by members of the SA and other nationalist groups, a Protestant rector blesses Nazi flags in late 1934. Stung by the resistance of some clergy, Reich Church leaders insisted that pastors take the same vow of obedience to Hitler sworn by soldiers and civil servants.

mythology, and a ritual exchange of bread and salt. Celebrants at SS "christenings" professed belief in the "mission of our German blood."

These ceremonies, and similar ones sponsored by the Nazi party, proved more popular among those who aspired to high places in the regime than among the population as a whole. To be sure, Hitler was idolized by millions of Germans. But his cult was based more on worldly accomplishments and hopes than on mystical indoctrination. Germany's dramatic economic recovery led many of those who had suffered through the depression to regard Hitler as their savior—a conviction that was bolstered in the late 1930s by his stunning diplomatic and military successes. This willingness of Germans to worship the Führer did not necessarily imply a

A young devotee of Hitler places flowers before his image in 1935. Such "Hitler corners," found in many German homes, were regarded as good-luck charms. During the war, it was claimed a wall graced with his portrait would withstand a bomb blast.

rejection of traditional religious customs. In fact, church attendance rose in Germany during the 1930s.

The most dramatic example of the persistence of religious traditions in the Reich was offered by the group that stood at greatest risk, the Jews. Hitler's rise to power and the state-sponsored actions against Jews that had followed, including boycotts of businesses, led to a revival of religious feeling among many Jews who had previously identified with their country more than with their faith. Synagogues were filled to overflowing, and despite the presence of Gestapo agents at services, rabbis heartened their congregations with references to the evils overcome by Jews in biblical times. A selection of psalms issued by Jewish philosopher Martin Buber in 1936 included the defiant passage, "Be Thou my judge, O God, and plead my cause against an ungodly nation."

Not surprisingly, when the Nazi leaders resolved in 1938 to declare outright war on the Jews, the synagogues were among their prime targets. On the night of November 9, bands of Nazi loyalists—including elements of the SS, SA, and Hitler Youth—sacked Jewish communities throughout Germany and Austria. The pogrom would come to be remembered as *Kristallnacht*, or the Night of Broken Glass. Hundreds of synagogues went up in flames as firefighters looked on, their only duty being to ensure that the fire did not spread. That night, more than 100 Jews were killed, and 30,000 were carted off to concentration camps. The next morning, those remaining to pick up the pieces tried to restore a semblance of order to their pillaged stores and homes. But in most places, the houses of worship that had kept alive their collective hope of deliverance lay in rubble. In a meeting a few days later, Propaganda Minister Joseph Goebbels, who had helped coordinate the violence at Hitler's behest, boasted, "In almost all German cities, the synagogues are burned." He hastened to add that the Jews would be allowed no chance to restore their temples: "We shall build parking lots in their places."

The savagery of *Kristallnacht* was felt even in the normally placid suburb of Eichkamp, where the Krugers and their neighbors were forced to confront the evidence. Horst, then in his late teens, walked past the shattered windows of Jewish-owned stores "in embarrassment and silence." That night, he recalled, there were "thoughtful faces at home, silent indignation: Does the Führer know about this?"

Neither the Krugers nor the millions of other law-abiding Germans who had put their faith in Hitler cared to ponder that question for long. It was easier to blame the misdeeds on overzealous Storm Troopers or Gestapo agents. Most Germans continued to echo the sentiments of a devout woman in Eichkamp, who remarked to Horst Kruger, "What, you don't believe the Führer was sent to us by God?" Only the crushing lessons of military defeat would destroy such conviction.

Kruger saw his mother and father for the last time late in the eleventh of the Reich's twelve years. He was by then a soldier, home briefly on leave. "They had become frighteningly old; for four years of war, they had lived exclusively off ration coupons, and now even their expressions were exhausted, rationed. They were like addicts suffering abrupt withdrawal from morphine: shaky and collapsed. My mother, who all through the years of greatness had dyed her hair a handsome black, had now turned snow white and was genuinely devout. And my father, who had never understood these worshipful attitudes, no longer understood anything at all, was at his wit's end, just kept shaking his head. All he did was moan softly, 'The bastards, the criminals, what have they done to us?' " ✚

Hitler Youth: Pitching Hay and Hand Grenades

To the casual observer, Germany's Hitler Youth seemed much like the scouting movements that flourished in other countries—tanned youngsters hiking, camping, and lifting their voices in song. But in fact it was a government-dominated organization dedicated to making fervent Nazis of the nation's children and producing obedient, savage warriors for the Third Reich.

The Hitler Youth was vast, pervasive, and relentless in its propaganda. By 1938, its combined boys' and girls' divisions claimed eight million members—or more than 90 percent of all young people aged ten and older. Companies and battalions were active in every town and city. Even the Jungvolk, the ten- to fourteen-year-old members, learned close-order drill, paraded on Nazi holidays, and heard long speeches deifying Hitler. "He who serves the Führer serves Germany, and

whoever serves Germany serves God," proclaimed Baldur von Schirach, who ran the entire program.

The older members went on route marches and camping trips organized like army bivouacs. They also worked hard on farms to ease the labor shortage, and as war approached, they learned to shoot rifles and hurl grenades. The program's overriding purpose, Hitler declared, was to brainwash the nation's youth to "think German, act German," and then fill the ranks of the Wehrmacht, the SS, and the almost equally regimented labor force. "They will never be free," he noted with satisfaction, "for the rest of their lives."

Hitler Youths build a haystack under a farmer's watchful eye. Launched in 1934, the farm-duty program was intended to harden the youngsters; instead, the sixty-hour workweeks often damaged their health and interfered with their education.

Playing a popular game called Roman chariot, competing Hitler Youth teams emulate horses and charioteers at camp in 1933.

Below, ten-year-old Jungvolk, mustered in front of their tents, execute a reasonably disciplined "eyes left" during a Hitler Youth encampment at Berlin's Tempelhof airfield in 1934.

War Games for Ten-Year-Olds

"Campfires, cookouts, Indian games, and adventurous field trips: All this made the Hitler Youth so attractive," recalled a former member, Fritz Langour, who eagerly joined the Jungvolk in 1937, at the age of ten. Even more exciting, he remembered, were the war games—learning infantry tactics, camouflage, how to plot an enemy position with map and compass. Children who became proficient at such tasks, Langour also recalled, were given "a sharp dagger, a side arm in miniature—a weapon."

Two Jungvolk receive rifle instruction while older Hitler Youths practice the manual of arms in the background.

Training Tomorrow's Soldiers

After winning their daggers, the Jungvolk advanced to firing rifles and using gas masks. The eleven-year-olds began with air guns but were soon tutored on bolt-action .22s. By 1938, a million young Germans were taking part in marksmanship contests. Then came an even more warlike exercise—hurling dummy but realistic hand grenades *(next page).*

Becoming accustomed to wearing steel helmets and gas masks, three Jungvolk engage in a tug of war on a cobblestoned square in the old city of Worms.

At a sports festival, older members of the Hitler Youth show their skill throwing wooden sticks shaped like the army's potato-masher grenade.

In a test of courage, Hitler Youths leap over a bonfire *(right)* during a celebration of the summer solstice in 1937. Members of the Berlin youth group *(below)* carry a recumbent comrade in a simulated funeral. The other youngsters hold wooden swords and shields blazoned with the runic symbol used by the Hitler Youth and SS.

Learning to Die for the Führer

Beyond weapons training, the Hitler Youth also taught a generation of Germans to defy danger and glory in the idea of dying heroically in battle. Part of this psychological conditioning was imposed at nighttime ceremonies, such as those shown here, and at the huge annual rallies at Nuremberg *(next page)*.

Building on the German fondness for gathering around a bonfire, Youth Leader Schirach conceived neopagan ceremonies at which Hitler's young disciples recited verses, sang patriotic songs, and even performed mock funerals for "fallen comrades." The songs also celebrated death in combat. One that appeared in the Hitler Youth songbook for 1933 included the verse, "We fight for German honor. We die for Adolf Hitler." A popular slogan chanted by the members stated the message even more prophetically: "We are born to die for Germany."

Carrying distinctive Hitler Youth banners, teenage color-bearers pass the ranks of Nazi faithful at a Nuremberg party rally. Each year, one day of the massive demonstration was dedicated to the Hitler Youth, and tens of thousands marched in review before the Führer himself.

FOUR

The High Cost of Better Times

Two laborers who had been home for Easter boarded a train in the spring of 1936 to return to their jobs building the autobahn, Nazi Germany's emerging network of superhighways. Oblivious to the presence of two other persons in their compartment, the men grumbled about their work. It was backbreaking, they complained; the overseers drove them at a furious pace. The housing was wretched, the food bad, the pay inadequate. After deductions and so-called voluntary contributions to various Nazi agencies, they netted only sixteen reichsmarks, or less than seven dollars, a week—less than they had been earning six months earlier. After a time, a woman seated across the way looked up reprovingly from her newspaper. "Is this whining really necessary?" she asked. "You should be grateful that you have work and thank the Führer for getting rid of unemployment. In three years, Adolf Hitler has accomplished miracles, and from year to year things are getting better. You must have faith in the Führer."

Like virtually every aspect of life under the new order, construction of the autobahn was proving to be a double-edged sword. On the one hand, the project was a proud national achievement: Launched in 1933, it would create 2,000 miles of four-lane highways by 1938. By providing easy access to many cities, the roads would help unify the Reich. Just as important, building the autobahn was bolstering the economy by creating jobs for tens of thousands of unemployed men and by stimulating the growth of Germany's fledgling automobile industry.

The flip side was what bothered the two men on the train. The autobahn project was part of a revolution in values. Hitler was determined to mold the German people into a *Volksgemeinschaft,* or national community. In the Nazi lexicon, this meant that loyalty to the nation, and hence to the Führer, was the highest of all loyalties, above region, social class, church, even family. True, the workers had jobs, but their lives now resembled those of slave laborers more than those of free workers. There was also a sinister aspect to the project, although it was little recognized at the time. The new highways would enable the army to mobilize fast and efficiently, and their east-west axis would make a two-front war a manageable proposition.

Assembled along the Main River, newly hired laborers give the Nazi salute at groundbreaking ceremonies on September 23, 1933, for the first section of the autobahn, from Frankfurt to Heidelberg. Over the next two years, the project provided 84,000 jobs.

The fourth person in the compartment that day was a fifteen-year-old boy named Bernt Engelmann, who would recount the conversation years later. Engelmann himself would serve in another Nazi public-works program, the Reich Labor Service, known by its German initials RAD. The program required six months' service of every man between the ages of eighteen and twenty-five. (For women, the RAD was voluntary, but the pressure to join was intense.) The young men lived in labor camps and worked for subsistence wages at jobs such as farming, construction, and land reclamation. University and high-school graduates, craftsmen, peasants, and workers alike undertook the same menial tasks—part of Nazi policy to inculcate an "appropriate respect for manual labor." The regimented training and rugged conditions, it was hoped, would prepare the youths for war.

Through such projects as the autobahn and the Labor Service, Hitler was making good on his promises to end unemployment and solve Germany's farm crisis. By Easter of 1936, when young Engelmann overheard the conversation of the autobahn workers, only 1.8 million Germans were out of work, a dramatic reduction from the 6 to 8 million unemployed earlier in the depression. More and more people were saying, "The man may have his faults, but Hitler gave us a job and something to eat."

A high-speed, divided highway, the autobahn winds through the Werra Valley south of Northeim in this 1938 photograph. The road network's chief builder, Fritz Todt, shown receiving Hitler's congratulations *(inset)*, called his assignment an "artistic commission."

In the summer of 1936, Hitler wrote a memorandum that became the blueprint for the so-called Four-Year Plan, his ambitious scheme to achieve

national self-sufficiency. In it, the Führer spelled out his expansionist intentions. The plan would provide the economic muscle for gaining *Lebensraum,* the prewar slogan Hitler had appropriated for his claim to German living space in eastern Europe. "Economic rearmament," he wrote, "must be effected in the same tempo, with the same resolution, and if necessary with the same ruthlessness" as political and military rearmament. Hitler concluded his memorandum with a chilling command: "The German economy must be fit for war within four years."

Many of Hitler's financial advisers, including Hjalmar Schacht, the respected minister of economics, were appalled by the memorandum. Some critics privately called the resulting Four-Year Plan nothing less than a license to "strip-mine" the economy. But in the short run, the average citizen benefited. Under the impetus of the plan, with its emphasis on stepped-up rearmament, more and more Germans enjoyed a measure of prosperity. By 1938, jobs were so abundant that the Reich had to import workers. For the first time in a decade, Germans had security—but only at a price. Their taste of better times would cost them profoundly in lost freedoms, increased regimentation, and broken promises.

When Hitler took power in 1933, one of his foremost goals was to gain control of the German working class. The 15 million industrial workers who labored in factories, mines, and other blue-collar occupations undergirded the entire society. He needed their allegiance, or at least their acquiescence, if he was to revitalize the nation, rearm, and reach beyond its borders. As the name National Socialist German Workers' party attested, the Nazis had wooed the workers from the beginning but had made only minor inroads so far. Throughout the 1920s and early 1930s, industrial workers had remained loyal to their traditional trade unions and parties. The most radical among them were communists. Some belonged to the Catholic Center and other moderate parties. The great majority of organized labor, however, supported the Social Democrats, who had been responsible for the establishment of such fundamental privileges as collective bargaining and the right to strike.

The leftward tilt of labor galled Hitler—in his eyes it was all "Jewish Marxism"—and he was determined to crush the unions. He took the first steps in March of 1933, after the burning of the Reichstag building by a maverick Dutch anarchist provided him with a pretext. In scores of towns and cities, Storm Troopers shut down unions and occupied the offices of communist and socialist labor groups. Even after this crackdown, labor leaders continued to hope that their organizations could survive by cooperating with the new government.

Hitler buoyed these hopes by proclaiming May 1 the Day of National

Labor. Traditionally a special occasion in European countries, May Day had never been a national holiday in Germany. Now the Nazis stole the thunder of the Left—and deprived the unions of a potential focus for protests against the regime. Joseph Goebbels's Propaganda Ministry organized celebrations all over the Reich. In Berlin alone, more than 1.5 million workers marched in a parade, and the Führer himself expounded upon the day's theme, "Honor work, and respect the worker."

The next morning, May 2, the hammer fell. Storm Troopers seized union halls, confiscated union property, and threw labor leaders in jail. The centrist unions disbanded under pressure. To make certain they did not regroup, the government handed down decrees forbidding the formation of trade unions and outlawing strikes. By one decree, the government appointed about a dozen regional trustees of labor to oversee the regulation of wage scales and other matters formerly handled in negotiations between the unions and management.

At the same time, however, Hitler saw the need for organizing workers into a single mass movement tightly controlled by the Nazis. He authorized the creation of the Deutsche Arbeitsfront (DAF), or German Labor Front, to encompass all workers except members of the civil service and eventually to include employers as well. Although the DAF initially had no formal connection with the party, it was closely linked through its new chief, Robert Ley, a longtime Nazi party boss.

An alcoholic and an eccentric, Ley was a forty-three-year-old Rhinelander who had been trained as a chemist. He had served as an airman during the war and later worked at the giant chemical combine, I. G. Farben, where he was fired for political extremism. He had joined the Nazi party at its low ebb in 1924 and became a close friend of Hitler, who appointed him gauleiter in Cologne. There he used the party newspaper to campaign virulently against Jewish merchants and financiers and to extort protection money from potential targets of his attacks. An unwavering Hitler loyalist, Ley was rewarded for his fealty; the Führer appointed him head of the so-called Political Organization of the party in 1932 and leader of the Labor Front in 1933. "I myself am a son of peasants and have known poverty," Ley told the workers. "I swear to you not only that we shall preserve everything you have, but that we shall extend the rights of the worker in order that he might enter the new National Socialist state as an equal and respected member of the nation."

Dissent against Nazi labor policies surfaced almost at once. Ironically, most of the trouble came from workers who belonged to the segment of the Labor Front known as the National Socialist Factory Cells Organization (NSBO), which had been the Nazis' labor organization. The group, which had formed in 1930, took its name from the cells of Nazi workers established at factories in Berlin and the Ruhr. Much of its ideological bent came from Gregor Strasser, the leader of the party's socialist wing whom Hitler deposed in 1932. The NSBO grew rapidly after the Nazi takeover and claimed more than one million members by August 1933.

Brawny workers march arm in arm in a 1933 poster publicizing the first May Day celebration under Hitler. Before they came to power, the Nazis had scorned the traditional Marxist labor day as the "world-failure holiday."

The group's radicals regarded themselves as the rightful leaders of the German Labor Front. They pushed hard for the traditional union powers now vested in the government-appointed trustees of labor, who by inclination and background favored management. The radicals' attempts to wring higher wages and other concessions triggered sharp quarrels with several of the trustees. In Silesia, NSBO elements staged a brief mutiny at a steelworks and sabotaged machines at a clay and stone factory. In Westphalia, the trustee's special deputy found the "spirit of pure class warfare" so prevalent that he had to threaten NSBO representatives with intervention by the Gestapo.

Ley sympathized with the aims of the radicals, largely because he coveted the enormous power inherent in negotiating wages and working conditions. But Germany's leading industrialists had other ideas. They wanted to neutralize the working class. Hitler needed the cooperation of the industrialists for rearmament, so he went along with their antilabor stance. In November 1933, the Führer compelled Ley to sign an agreement curbing the powers of the Labor Front. Instead of deciding the "material questions of daily working life," the DAF would engage only in education and indoctrination, endeavoring "to educate all Germans who are at work to support the National Socialist state and to indoctrinate them in the National Socialist mentality." Old-line NSBO members were forced to the background. As Ley realistically explained to an audience of workers, "We are all soldiers of labor—some of us command and others obey."

Under terms of the agreement, which became law in January 1934, overall regulation of wages and working conditions remained in the hands of the labor trustees. But in the factory itself, day-to-day labor relations followed a system dear to the hearts of Nazi ideologues—the so-called *Führerprinzip*, or leadership principle; the employer was the leader and the workers his followers. In determining plant rules, the employer might consult with an advisory council of workers nominated by the Labor Front and elected

by the followers. But he had the final say, which was subject only to the council's appeal to the labor trustee. The trustee could refer abuses of authority by the employer or misdeeds by his worker-followers to so-called Courts of Social Honor—composed of a judge, an employer, and a worker from an advisory council.

From the worker's standpoint, the advisory councils were a shabby substitute for the trade-union mechanisms of pre-Nazi days. Although Ley hailed the annual elections of council members as the "freest and most incorruptible in the world," the balloting enjoyed less than enthusiastic participation. Encouraged by the remaining members of the Social Democratic party, many of whom had formed underground units after their party was outlawed, so many workers boycotted the elections in 1935 that the regime abolished the balloting and simply let the employers fill vacancies on the councils as they occurred.

Similarly, the Courts of Social Honor proved ineffectual. In 1935, of the 223 cases heard, 205 were against employers. Most of the defendants were small-business owners or artisans. The violations included some glaring instances of injustice, such as the physical abuse of apprentices. Yet only 9 of the employers suffered the severest punishment—loss of the right to run their businesses. And despite a sea of grievances that would have inundated the agenda of any legitimate union, the directors of the large factories were rarely called to defend themselves in the courts of honor.

Banned from operating as a traditional union, the Labor Front plunged into its assigned role of education and indoctrination. Ley started numerous programs to promote productivity and divert the workers' attention from their loss of freedom. Because employers were only too happy to cooperate with labor trustees in keeping the lid on wages, the average factory worker in 1936 earned thirty-five marks, or fourteen dollars, a week, a slight improvement over 1933 but well below predepression earnings. The higher pay resulted more from longer workdays than from increased hourly rates. Moreover, deductions for taxes, Labor Front dues, and obligatory contributions to party charities shrank take-home pay by about 18 percent. These increased deductions, together with rises in the cost of living estimated at 10 percent a year, meant a decline in actual purchasing power. Even in 1937, with conditions approaching full employment, earnings were so stagnant that more than 10 million people—one in six Germans—still qualified for parcels or subsidies from the Nazi charity, Winter Relief.

Following his own aphorism "It is more important to feed the souls of men than their stomachs," Ley tried to substitute psychological incentives for decent wages. One of his tactics was to elevate the workers' feelings of

German Labor Front leader Robert Ley *(center)* receives a hero's welcome on his return to Berlin from the 1933 International Workers' Conference in Geneva. Actually, the other participants had voted to unseat the Nazi delegation, and a French delegate called Ley the "prison warden of the German unions."

status by promoting the myth of a classless society. At Ley's instigation, for example, the Nazi-controlled press paid tribute to what it called the "peerage of hard jobs" by interviewing garbage collectors. Ley also encouraged employers and employees to wear the same simple blue uniform in the shop and recommended the abolition of the time clock. Instead of punching in at the beginning of the shift, blue-collar workers would attend a propaganda rally with their supervisors.

Another Ley project, dubbed Beauty of Labor, pressed employers to boost morale by improving the workers' physical surroundings. Beauty of Labor cadres pushed for better lighting, shower rooms, and canteens with inexpensive hot meals. The organization conducted a nationwide competition in which employers vied for recognition as the best of workplaces. Some companies built athletic fields and swimming pools for their employees. Going beyond physical amenities, a Cologne engine factory introduced an honor system in which the most reliable workers inspected their own work. The company designated especially energetic workers as "self-calculators," authorizing them to set their own piecework rates—ultimately at the expense of slower workers who could not keep pace.

The Labor Front assumed a central role in job training. It established training centers and, in collaboration with the Hitler Youth, sponsored an annual National Vocational Contest. Open to young men and women between the ages of fifteen and twenty-one who belonged to any Nazi

organization, the competition tested practical skills in a score of different vocations. Entrants also took written examinations in arithmetic and composition and in so-called political theory—meaning Nazi ideology. The political portion of the examinations inspired an oft-quoted story about a hairdresser's assistant who proudly announced that she had no problems with shampooing, waving, and dyeing but could not "keep from mixing up Göring's and Goebbels's birthdays."

The contest became immensely popular, attracting more than 3.5 million entrants by 1939. Winners at the local level moved on to regional competitions for the right to participate in the national championships in Berlin and five other major cities. The grand winners were treated like celebrities—photographed for the newspapers, interviewed on the radio, and invited to have tea with Ley and the Führer himself. The contest was hailed as a triumph of the Nazi emphasis on vocational training; about 80 percent of the winners had failed as children to gain acceptance into secondary schools that would have allowed them to continue in higher education.

Under a poster promoting a one-pot supper—the term used to urge Germans to conserve by eating frugally at least one day a week—an official of Winter Relief, the Nazis' annual charity drive, issues a collection tin to a Hitler Youth. With the help of voluntary contributions, the Nazis provided hot meals for the needy, including the 2,000 hungry Berliners being served in Deutschland Hall *(right)*.

The Labor Front's ultimate morale-building effort was the vast program of leisure activities and mass tourism known as Kraft durch Freude, or Strength through Joy. Widely referred to by the initials of its German name, KdF, and modeled after an existing program in fascist Italy, it was launched in late 1933 with funds confiscated from the defunct trade unions and was later financed by Labor Front dues. The name came from the notion that after participating in the joy of regimented leisure, the worker would return to the job with new strength. A DAF press officer put it more crudely, likening the worker to the "engine of a motor vehicle that must be overhauled after it has done a certain number of kilometers."

Most of the KdF's programs were copied directly from the disbanded unions and simply given a Nazi tinge. It offered adults courses ranging from English and French to shorthand and algebra, and propaganda forums on subjects such as race and heredity. It sponsored sports programs, constructed libraries, staged amateur theatricals, and provided inexpensive tickets to professional concerts and plays. In 1938, KdF-subsidized cultural events attracted nearly 20 million workers and other Germans.

The most highly praised programs enabled workers to get away from it all. On one-day outings arranged by the KdF travel bureau, workers could bicycle, ski, or hike. They could take weekend trips to the Black Forest by chartered train. Or they could spend a week's vacation in the Harz Mountains for just twenty-eight marks, less than a week's wages for most people. So many workers availed themselves of these vacation journeys, short trips, and outings—more than 10 million in 1938—that some rural innkeepers posted signs saying "Not Visited by KdF" in order to retain their upper-crust clientele, who might not be enamored of the "classless" society.

Particularly appealing to blue-collar workers were cruises on the KdF's fleet of twelve ocean liners. In 1938, these ships carried 131,623 Labor Front members on cut-rate holidays to tourist meccas from the Norwegian fjords to the balmy islands of the Mediterranean Sea—fantasy trips previously beyond the reach of most Germans. These vacations were more expensive —the longer ones might cost more than a typical month's wages—and

were limited to members selected for their hard work and loyalty to the Nazi party. As a result, working-class people on a cruise were usually outnumbered by higher-paid craftsmen, white-collar workers, and supervisors. But everyone aboard ship, including the crew, traveled in the same single-class accommodations.

In addition to their popularity with workers, KdF programs yielded secondary benefits for the Nazis. They stimulated the tourist economy by filling up trains, hotels, and restaurants. They promoted the notion of a national community by enabling all kinds of Germans to see their country and to mingle with one another. And they allowed the regime to burnish its image in other European countries by showing off legions of sun-tanned and presumably happy Germans on holiday.

The winners of the National Vocational Contest at the *kreis*, or local, level received this badge. The eagle holds in its talons a bronze gearwheel, the emblem of the Labor Front, and the diamond-shaped insignia of the Hitler Youth.

Thanks to Strength through Joy and other thriving enterprises, the Labor Front grew into a potent force. Besides the fleet of cruise ships, its empire embraced banks, insurance companies, publishing firms, and housing associations. The DAF's 25 million members made it by far the largest organization in the Reich—and the richest. In 1939, membership dues amounted to 539 million reichsmarks, or 216 million dollars. By now formally affiliated with the Nazi party, the Labor Front was the party's largest source of funds and jobs. Its payroll of 44,500 employees was bloated with old-line Nazi functionaries too incompetent to work in the party bureaucracy, and the front's activities were riddled with corruption. Ley presided over it all, constantly shuffling people and paper to satisfy what one rival called his "gigantomania." He enjoyed the work immensely—and lined his pockets with a verve that scandalized even the Nazis. Ley and his beautiful young second wife Inge divided their time among half a dozen luxurious mansions staffed by armies of servants provided by the DAF.

During the late 1930s, however, the Labor Front's mission of helping regiment workers while keeping them reasonably productive became increasingly difficult. The problem arose as early as 1936, when Hitler intensified the pace of rearmament. The arms industry eventually absorbed the remaining million unemployed workers and grew so robustly that, by the end of 1938, Germany faced an overall shortage of one million laborers.

Employers had to compete for skilled workers, especially in the sorely pressed metal and building industries. To keep business humming, managers offered higher wages and generous fringe benefits. During the three years before the war, weekly earnings in industry went up an average of 17 percent, although much of this was attributable to the virtual abandonment of the eight-hour workday. Switching jobs to earn more became so commonplace that German workers, who at one time might have kept the

same job for life, were moving on an average of once every twelve months.

These manifestations of the law of supply and demand were anathema to the Nazis. Higher wages drove up costs of consumer goods and weapons, and chronic job-changing disrupted factory production. The regime responded by imposing restrictions on movement between jobs, but labor-starved employers helped workers evade the law. Then, in June 1938, the government tightened the screws. Hermann Göring, who had been appointed director of the Four-Year Plan, authorized labor trustees to fix maximum rates of pay for various skills and later ordered the trustees to limit fringe benefits as well. He also decreed the drafting of workers for key military projects, notably the construction of the West Wall, or so-called Siegfried Line, along the frontier with France. This project almost immediately resulted in the conscription of more than 300,000 men to serve under Fritz Todt, the former chief of autobahn construction, and only made the labor shortage worse.

Some workers, spurred by the socialist and communist underground, reacted to the stepped-up regimentation with surprising militancy. They staged slowdowns, stayed home from work, and daubed anti-Nazi slogans on factory walls. At the I. G. Farben factory in Wolfen, workers felt so confident of their power—600 positions were unfilled there—that a few brazenly took afternoons off to attend the cinema or returned drunk from tea breaks. In Berlin, wives demonstrated at railroad stations as their husbands were transported away to build the West Wall. In the factories, there were even occasional strikes. The Labor Front recorded 192 work stoppages during one eighteen-month period. Some strikes resulted from friction between Nazi overseers and workers, but in at least one instance, Nazis joined in. Most strikes did not involve many workers—typically fewer than thirty took part—and were quickly ended by the intervention of party officials or the Gestapo.

No large-scale uprisings occurred. The vast majority of Germans were too happy to have a job, too weary from long hours of work, or too afraid to act. It was this last factor, the palpable aura of terror and intimidation, that underlay the labor policies of the Third Reich. The Labor Front shop steward, along with such happier duties as arranging Strength through Joy holidays, was concerned above all with keeping tabs on the workers' loyalty—and calling in the Gestapo when it turned sour.

Unlike the workers, with their history of loyalty to the left-wing Social Democrats, Germany's more than four million merchants and self-employed craftsmen gravitated naturally to the Nazi party. Early on, this element of the middle class had been attracted by the movement's radical

With a woman on each arm, Robert Ley strolls the deck of a cruise ship for workers. "Strength through Joy is very popular," wrote one observer. "The events appeal to the yearning of the little man who wants an opportunity to share in the pleasures of the 'top people'."

German tourists get acquainted with a young ice-cream vendor in Madeira. Although a Strength through Joy package tour to the Portuguese island in 1938 cost only 155 reichsmarks, or about 62 dollars, barely one in 200 workers could afford the trip.

economic doctrines, which denounced investment capital and interest payments as forms of slavery and advocated nationalizing the banks and other agencies of high finance. Fiercely antiunion and anticommunist, the shopkeepers, shoemakers, and carpenters also detested such institutions of modern industrial society as mass-production factories, department stores, and consumer cooperatives, which threatened their existence. They believed the Nazis' promise to restore small businesses to their place of privilege in the community.

"I was pinning all my hopes on the Nazis, because our business was on the verge of collapse," recalled a party member whose shop specialized in electrical appliances and phonograph records. "They had a program that sounded perfect. They called it 'breaking the tyranny of investment capital,' which meant expropriating the department stores and renting out the space at low rates to small-business owners. That would have saved us, because the cheap light bulbs in Woolworth's and the popular records at rock-bottom prices in the department stores were stealing our customers."

In December 1932, only a few weeks before Hitler became chancellor, shopkeepers and craftsmen within the party organized the Fighting League of Middle-Class Tradespeople. The following spring, in concert with another Nazi retail association, local party officials, and contingents of Storm Troopers, the league launched a campaign to control economic life in the towns and cities. The alliance took over local chambers of commerce and handicraft guilds, pushed through ordinances to shut down restaurants in department stores, and, in one town where the commissioner of the licensing bureau happened to own a gardening-equipment store, enjoined Woolworth's from selling garden tools.

In April and May of 1933, Nazi tradesmen undertook their most ambitious troublemaking by conducting nationwide boycotts of Jewish businesses, department stores, and consumer cooperatives. They had the encouragement of the party's economics chief, Otto Wagener. A forty-five-year-old one-time businessman and former chief of staff of the Storm Troopers, Wagener had succeeded Strasser as the symbol of the socialist wing of the Nazi movement. Wagener was a confidant of Hitler, however, and the Führer himself supported the boycotts.

Party leaders quickly had second thoughts about the implications of such disruptions. At a time when Hitler was trying to revive Germany's depressed economy, destruction of the department stores threatened to throw thousands of employees onto the streets and jeopardize the jobs of many more workers at the stores' suppliers. Banks that had backed the big stores with loans also stood to lose. Hitler became so concerned about the impact on the economy that, at the end of June, he agreed to invest 14.5 million reichsmarks—4.2 million dollars—of the government's money to prevent the collapse of the Hertie department-store chain and the loss of

Women at a Nuremberg toy factory pack miniature trains for the 1934 Christmas season. As Hitler's rearmament program accelerated, thousands of women abandoned such occupations for better-paying jobs in heavy industry and weapons plants.

14,000 jobs. He acted even though its owners were Jewish and the chain had recently been a special target of the league's boycott.

This decision signaled the Führer's turn from ideology to pragmatism in economic matters. He feared that radical experiments could create chaos and get in the way of his courtship of big business. Soon he fired Wagener, whose anticapitalist fervor had alienated the industrialists, and replaced him with a man more acceptable to them. (Wagener, who would narrowly escape being murdered in the Blood Purge of June 1934, found a new career in the army.) Hitler had his deputy, Rudolf Hess, order the Fighting League of Middle-Class Tradespeople and other Nazi organizations to drop their campaign against the department stores. Shortly afterward, the league was dissolved and its remnants absorbed into the German Labor Front.

The regime could not completely ignore the demands of small business, however. Merchants and artisans represented not only the nucleus of the party but also a significant segment of the national economy. Handicrafts alone accounted for about 10 percent of all sales, and the Reich's 540,000 small retailers played key roles in distributing consumer goods. To help the small operators survive, Hitler imposed a law reducing by half the number of large consumer cooperatives, which operated all kinds of businesses, from butcher shops to construction firms. He also banned the establishment of new department stores and the expansion of existing ones, and prohibited them from providing services such as shoe repair and barbering. The opening of any new retail store was at first forbidden and later allowed only by official permit. This enabled the trade itself to police competition through the organization that approved such applications.

Craftsmen also won some of their longtime demands. Carpenters and others in the construction trades profited from government subsidies for the renovation of housing and from Hitler's program to create massive new edifices at Nuremberg *(pages 44-51)* and elsewhere for the greater glory of the Reich. Existing craft guilds were given new powers that enabled them to make membership compulsory, discipline their members, fix prices, and take substantial control of apprenticeship programs. Because would-be artisans now had to pass a guild-administered test of professional skills and "political suitability," the number of new competitors decreased. Courts of honor composed of guild members intervened in cases of price-cutting and other unethical practices. The regime also expanded the craft guild system to embrace such hitherto-neglected entrepreneurs as street vendors and fairground exhibitors.

Despite such gains, it soon became obvious that small retailers and craftsmen, their loyalty to Nazi ideology notwithstanding, were the regime's poor relations. The Labor Front absorbed the remaining coopera-

tives and kept them operating. The big department stores weathered their crises and prospered. When they and other retailers that were owned by Jews underwent the process of Aryanization—the Nazi euphemism for expropriation by the state or party—most of the stores wound up in the hands of major business concerns rather than small retailers. The combined sales of cooperatives and department stores continued to exceed those of the smaller retailers.

At the same time, new government regulations got in the way. The state imposed uniform accounting procedures on small-business owners and pored over their books to ensure the payment of taxes. Butchers and greengrocers were squeezed between the prices they had to pay the farmer and the price ceilings imposed by the state. Some shops resorted to a system of double prices. The side of the tag with the higher price was for the customer; the other side was for the benefit of government snoops.

Small businesses suffered most as rearmament pumped new life into the economy in the late 1930s. Artisans had to compete with heavy industry for scarce raw materials and labor. Shoemakers could not buy enough leather, nor carpenters lumber, and merchants watched their clerks desert them for better pay in the factories. By 1939, the government was forcibly shutting down nonessential businesses in order to free up labor—"reducing the bloated apparatus of the distribution trade," as the SS newspaper *The Black Corps* put it. The fate of retailers who sold radios was typical of the resulting decline among merchants: The number of radio dealers plummeted by more than half during the first six years of Nazi rule. Their demise was hastened by a brainstorm from propaganda maestro Goebbels. He decided that the government should mass-produce inexpensive radios so more people could listen directly to the Führer. The number of self-employed artisans also shrank dramatically—nearly 10 percent, from 1.65 to 1.5 million, between 1936 and 1939.

The survivors of this shakeout now had a slightly larger slice of the economic pie, but their share of the profits could not approach that of big business. Merchants and artisans continued to complain so vocally that a secret report to the Social Democrats in exile called them the "main body of grumblers and discontents." Still, their grievances tended to be economic, not political, and small-business owners remained the backbone of the Nazi regime's support.

The other mainstay of the German middle class, the farmer, also enlisted in the new order with high hopes. In Hitler's ranking of economic priorities early in 1933, the revival of agriculture shared top billing with the relief of unemployment. Nearly 30 percent of the population worked in agriculture,

and most of the Reich's three million farms were locked in the grip of the price collapse brought on by worldwide depression. Burdened by debt that consumed one-sixth of their income in interest payments, most farmers still plowed their fields with oxen and tied their bundles of grain by hand. They lived very simply: Only one in three German farms had running water.

The exceptions to this bleak picture were the landed gentry of East Prussia known as Junkers. These aristocratic families, which for centuries had provided the nucleus of the German army's officer corps, controlled most of the large estates—250 acres or more—that composed one-sixth of the Reich's arable land. The Junkers had weathered the depression thanks to huge government subsidies granted during the last years of the Weimar Republic. Feudal tradition as well as wealth set the Junkers apart from the peasant farmers. It was still common practice, for example, for farm hands to kiss the hem of a Junker's coat when greeting him.

To change all this—to step up food production and promote the stature of the ordinary farmer—Hitler turned to a former pig breeder named Richard-Walther Darré. Born of German parents in Argentina in 1895, Darré had served as a lieutenant of field artillery during the war, then studied agronomy and animal husbandry. In a series of books and pamphlets, Darré brewed a hodgepodge of anti-Semitic racism and back-to-the-land romanticism that came to be known as *Blut und Boden,* or blood and soil. He believed that members of the so-called Nordic race were the originators of European culture and that the German peasant was their rightful heir.

Darré's mystical idealization of the peasant way of life profoundly influenced at least two Nazi leaders. Heinrich Himmler became a believer; later, as chief of the SS, he would apply the twisted notion of racial purity in the extermination camps of Germany and eastern Europe. Hitler, too, was taken by Darré's vision of a peasant aristocracy—"the new peerage of blood and soil"—and in 1930 appointed him director of the party's agrarian section. Until then, the Nazis had paid little attention to the peasants. But under Darré, the party gained a measure of electoral support in the countryside and infiltrated the leadership of the largest farm organizations.

In June 1933, Hitler named Darré to the cabinet as minister of agriculture. Darré succeeded Alfred Hugenberg, the Nationalist party leader whom Hitler had appointed to the twin posts of agriculture and economics in order to secure the necessary Nationalist support in the Reichstag. After Hitler had crippled the Reichstag in March, he no longer needed Hugenberg, and the Nazi-controlled farm organizations provided the pretext for getting rid of him by staging demonstrations in support of Darré.

In his new post, and with the additional party title of Reich peasant leader, Darré presided over policies aimed at sheltering farms from the forces of the free market. The goals of these policies often were contradictory. Darré wanted to improve the prices paid to farmers, for example, and at the same time hold down the cost of food to consumers. He wanted to preserve the traditional peasant way of life while simultaneously stimulating agricultural production.

The two cornerstones of the new order in farming were laid in September 1933, within three months of Darré's appointment. The first was a law that sought to "retain the peasantry as the blood spring of the German nation." To prevent land speculation and protect the farmer from the free market, it designated as hereditary farms all holdings between 18 and 300 acres in size—about one-fifth of German farms. The law relieved the hereditary farm of a substantial portion of any existing debt but tightly circumscribed its future. Upon the death of the owner, the holding would pass undivided to the eldest son. None of the land could be sold or mortgaged, and no creditor could foreclose.

The owner of the hereditary farm became the subject of special ideological attention. He was entitled to be called *Bauer,* the German word for peasant, which now became a Nazi honorific. All other people engaged in agriculture, whether their holdings were larger or smaller, were relegated to the status of mere *Landwirte,* or farmers. The peasant and his family underwent physical examinations and were asked to provide their family history to authorities. The objective was to determine if the peasant would produce healthy offspring to go with his bumper crops and scientifically bred livestock—as well as to prevent Jews from owning farmland.

The other cornerstone of Nazi farm policy was the Reich Food Estate, which was established to control production, prices, and distribution. Theoretically an autonomous public corporation but in fact linked to party and state at every level, the Food Estate's jurisdiction encompassed every aspect of agriculture. Its compulsory membership comprised not only the Reich's three million farms but also 42,000 agricultural cooperatives; dairies, mills, and other processors employing some 300,000 workers; and 500,000 retail food stores. In return for guaranteeing prices, the Food Estate told the farmer what to raise, how much, and when and where to deliver it. Relevant data was recorded in a dossier maintained for each farm and updated monthly. A farmer who failed to hew to the line faced a fine or imprisonment.

Farm women wearing peasant costumes show off sheafs of grain at the Nazi regime's first Harvest Thanksgiving Day in October 1933. Minister of Agriculture Walther Darré *(left)* linked Hitler with the successful harvest by referring to him as the Peasant Chancellor.

All this planning, monitoring, and enforcement required a human apparatus of 70,000 employees staffing offices at the local, district, state, and national levels. Unlike the Labor Front and other bloated Nazi bureaucracies, the Food Estate proved to be reasonably cost-effective. More than three-fourths of the staff were unpaid volunteers—typically Nazi farmers—who served as local *Bauernführer*, or peasant leaders. Besides the full-time job of running his own farm, the peasant leader had to worry about his neighbors. His long list of duties included such disparate chores as monitoring political attitudes, conducting indoctrination meetings for rural women, checking cattle for disease, and making sure that hens met their annual production quota of precisely sixty-five eggs.

In addition to sustaining prices and preserving the family farm through the heredity law, the Nazis gave special attention to enhancing the dignity of rural life. Every autumn, they held Harvest Thanksgiving Day, a festival that attracted close to one million farm folk to the city of Hameln to hear the Führer praise the peasantry as the "future of the nation." Many of the farmers wore traditional costumes handsewn for the occasion. In the countryside, representatives of the Food Estate's Department of Peasant Culture revived old traditions and invented new customs, such as a ceremony to mark the handing down of the family farm to the heir and new *Bauer*. In keeping with Darré's notions, Food Estate agents even fostered

rural heraldry by encouraging farmers to submit family coats of arms—most of which turned out to be bogus crests created by companies eager to exploit the "new aristocracy."

Farmers savored all the fuss made over them but counted their blessings as mixed. They frequently complained about the regime's intrusion into the freedom and individuality they had long prized. For example, the hereditary-farm law so tied the hands of the peasants that they felt like mere administrators of their land, rather than true owners. No longer allowed to mortgage their farms, they had a hard time getting credit. And

Shouldering their shovels like weapons, Labor Service youths leave camp for a day's work building a road high in the Alps. "They were in splendid health," an American visitor reported, "and were kept too busy to have time to criticize."

they worried that their daughters and younger sons would be unable to continue the family way of life, especially since the price of land not covered by the law was escalating rapidly. The primacy law, in fact, turned out to be so unpopular that almost one-third of the eligible farmers asked to have their land excluded from it.

Many other constraints imposed by the Food Estate rankled the country folk. Some farmers circumvented flour-quality requirements by mixing in inferior grades; others sold their cattle to dealers at illegal prices. Farmers also grumbled about regulations that made them market milk to intermediaries instead of directly to the public. These rules idled their butter-making apparatus and forced them to buy back as skim milk what they needed for their own use. Others complained that they had to work harder than anyone else in the Reich. After hearing his fill of such complaints, a local Nazi leader wrote, "The peasant is of such a disposition that he thinks only he has to work and the others earn their money for nothing."

For a time, farmers were better off economically under Hitler. During the first three years of his regime, farm income rose steadily—not to predepression levels, but at a faster rate than the rest of the economy. Special tax reductions and debt-relief measures allowed farmers to keep more of what they earned. In 1936, however, the growth of farm income began to lag behind trade and industry. Two years later, agriculture's share of the German economy dwindled to the point where it was actually less than when Hitler had taken office.

Like many merchants and craftsmen, the peasantry was victimized by the prosperity that was brought on by rearmament. While the government generally froze the prices of foodstuffs, farmers had to pay higher production costs, especially for labor—if they could find workers at all. More and more farm hands moved to factory and construction jobs that paid higher wages for less work. They were drawn to cities that offered better housing and such urban amenities as shops, cafés, and movie houses. By harvesttime in 1937, German farms were almost 400,000 pairs of hands short of what was needed.

Although the flight from the land occurred in all industrialized nations, it reached crisis proportions in the Third Reich. Between 1933 and 1939, an estimated 1.5 million Germans—12.5 percent of the rural population—left the farm. This total included not only laborers and their families but also the officially honored peasants—and their wives and children. Young women, after watching their mothers work themselves to death, wanted to marry soldiers or industrial workers—anyone but a farmer. ("Nowadays, they would rather wear silk stockings than clogs," said a farmer's wife.) Some heirs, sadly aware that the farm they inherited could not reap enough

profit to buy a tractor or hire labor, simply abandoned their birthright and moved to the city or joined the army.

Darré and his ideologues tried desperately to keep the vaunted peasants on their farms. They made it illegal for farm workers to leave without government permission. But after two years, the prohibition was suspended. Too many young people simply refused to be trapped in dead-end agricultural jobs when the higher pay and increasingly acute labor needs of industry beckoned. Darré introduced special vocational training and farm apprenticeships, but in 1937 only 7,000 of 41,000 available slots were filled. The Labor Front tried to help by providing cultural and sports programs, but farmers who had to spend two hours a day operating a pump just to produce running water had little interest in such diversions.

Failing to stem the tide away from the farm, the regime devised various stopgaps. Conscripts from the Reich Labor Service, volunteers from the League of German Girls and Hitler Youth, and young women fulfilling their so-called duty year for the fatherland—all served time harvesting grain, milking cows, and generally easing the burden on the hard-pressed peasant family. Darré hoped the youngsters would find the experiences so exhilarating that many would permanently opt for the rural life, but few did. The most successful program—a voluntary influx of Italians, Poles, and other foreign workers—also proved the most worrisome to the Nazis. These seasonal helpers were not only reliable workers but eligible mates for young farm women whose potential husbands had decamped for the cities. In the view of the ideological faithful, the resulting crossbreeding threatened to adulterate the precious "blood spring of the German nation."

Neither the flight from the land nor other agricultural developments had much impact on the Junker estates. At first, the regime had made much of a scheme to enlarge the peasantry by creating new farms in the underpopulated eastern areas where the landed gentry held sway. By one calculation, carving up the estates would have resulted in 250,000 new holdings. For all their talk, however, the Nazis resorted to reclamation and purchase—not expropriation—to form 20,748 medium-size farms. The total was little more than half of the new holdings that had been developed under the Weimar Republic.

The Nazi regime left the large estates and the Junker way of life relatively untouched. One reason was a reluctance to expropriate big farms that could afford labor and machinery and thus were highly productive. Another was the need to maintain amicable relations with the source of much of Germany's military leadership. In the years immediately ahead, twenty noble families from the east would contribute 160 members to the Wehrmacht general staff. The Junkers were able to carry on aristocratic pastimes;

"You must save five marks a week if you want to drive your own car!" reads this Strength through Joy poster, advertising the Volkswagen layaway plan.

Icons and Insignia for Everyone

Nazi Germany was a nation awash with posters and badges used to exhort the public and recognize individual participation in activities sanctioned by the government. No organization made better use of these two propaganda devices than Robert Ley's powerful German Labor Front (DAF), which produced literally thousands of each.

Labor Front posters, such as the one above showing a happy family behind the wheel of its own automobile, invariably portrayed idealized visions of life under Nazi rule. In addition to membership badges, the DAF commissioned insignia for every imaginable occasion, from Strength through Joy holidays to Labor Service rallies. These commemorative badges had the dual effect of making the event seem important and bonding the participants into a united front.

Posters and badges from the Labor Front and related agencies demonstrate their involvement in German life. The placard at left, showing workers touring the fjords, promises, "Now you too can travel!" Below, a donation cup for Winter Relief declares, "Workers collect, workers give!" At right, posters for the Labor Service (RAD) appeal to women ("RAD Leader—A Call of the

Times") and men ("We strengthen body and soul"). The badges at bottom identify *(left to right)* membership in the young women's RAD, attendance at an RAD sports meeting, men's RAD membership, Labor Front leader, attendance at the Volkswagen cornerstone laying, membership in the Nazi Factory Cells Organization, and a Strength through Joy cruise to Italy.

they still made nighttime forays into the forest in evening dress to hunt stag and other quarry on paths illuminated by the torches of foresters and beaters. In order to qualify for the necessary hunting license, however, they now had to become members of the Nazi Hunters' Association.

Meanwhile, after six years of Nazi rule, the noble peasants, pride of the blood-and-soil ideologues, were struggling. In 1939, many of them were working up to sixteen hours a day, three hours longer than they had a decade earlier. A report by the regime's own security service spoke of a "mood close to complete despair" in the countryside. "I know many farmers who haven't bought themselves a new Sunday suit for ten years," wrote one of the Food Estate's volunteer farm leaders. "In my district, I know scarcely two who have radios, and those are the ones whose sons or daughters work in factories."

From the standpoint of the average consumer—whether industrial worker, small-business owner, or farmer—the standard of living rose under the Nazis in comparison with the early depression years. Mainly because people worked longer hours, income increased during the late 1930s. And although prices also went up, Germans generally ate better and enjoyed access to more amusements, such as the movies. But the regime's attempt to produce both guns and butter often fell short on the consumer side of the ledger. For example, despite the creation of 300,000 new or renovated housing units a year, housing continued to be a major headache. One in three Germans lived in overcrowded or substandard conditions. The problem was particularly acute in rural areas and in small industrial cities, where the rearmament boom more than doubled the population. By 1938, the Reich urgently needed 1.5 million new dwellings.

Consumers endured, however, sometimes even with enthusiasm, because Nazi propaganda kept promising that things would get better. The classic instance of such a promise was the story of the little automobile known as the *Volkswagen,* or people's car. Automobile ownership in Germany was the prerogative of the wealthy; one in fifty Germans owned a car, compared with one in five Americans. But Hitler proposed to put the common man behind the wheel of a Volkswagen for only 990 reichsmarks, or 397 dollars—one-third the price Americans paid for a new car in 1939.

The Volkswagen was a work of both engineering and propaganda genius. A tiny, beetle-shaped vehicle with an air-cooled engine in the rear, it was the invention of Ferdinand Porsche, who had won international acclaim as the designer of elegant passenger and racing cars. Born in 1875 in the German Sudeten portion of what would later become Czechoslovakia, Porsche was a little man whose prim looks disguised a hot temper. He had

Hitler congratulates the 1938 winners of the German National Prize for Art and Science: from left, aircraft designers Ernst Heinkel and Willy Messerschmitt, Volkswagen manufacturer Ferdinand Porsche, and construction engineer Fritz Todt. Each received 100,000 reichsmarks and a decoration *(below)* featuring a profile of Athena, the Greek goddess of wisdom, on a star of platinum and gold.

scant formal education but a natural feel for mechanical design, and by the early 1920s he had dreamt of a small car that every person could afford. Because of that obsession—and his temper—he had left prestigious positions at Daimler and other big automakers in order to build experimental prototypes of the ideal car.

In 1934, when Porsche was almost sixty years old, his concept came to the attention of the man who could make it a reality. Hitler loved automobiles, especially big black Mercedes, although he never learned to drive. He was the first German politician to campaign extensively by automobile, and his passion for motoring led him as chancellor to fix upon the autobahn as his premier public-works project. At the 1933 Berlin Auto Show, he called upon industry to create a people's car, and his subsequent meeting with Porsche set the ambitious Volkswagen project in motion.

Porsche painstakingly crafted prototypes of the new car in the garage next to his house, then subjected Daimler-built models of the vehicle to more than a million miles of road-testing by SS drivers. Meanwhile, Hitler set out to exploit the project for maximum propaganda. When established automakers showed little enthusiasm for the idea, he turned to Ley and his dues-rich German Labor Front. Recalling Hitler's pledge to the people that the car would be the "source of yet-unknown happiness to them, on Sundays and holidays," Ley designated his leisure-time organization, Strength through Joy, sponsor of the Volkswagen.

The Labor Front formed a new company to build the car and developed production facilities. Planners selected a site east of Hanover known as Wolfsburg, after the medieval castle on one of the Junker estates that had to be expropriated for the project. The automotive complex covered twenty square miles; it was to include a mammoth factory capable of producing an unheard-of 1.5 million cars a year and a town housing 30,000 workers and their families. To learn mass-production methods, Porsche and some of his colleagues visited the United States, where they toured auto plants and talked with Henry Ford, whom the Nazi regime would soon decorate for his work in "giving autos to the masses." They also recruited a score of engineers and production specialists, German-born or of German descent, who agreed to return to the fatherland to help set up the assembly lines.

Amid great fanfare, Hitler laid the cornerstone for the Wolfsburg factory on May 26, 1938. He announced that the car would be named after the organization that sponsored it and that "works hardest to provide the broadest masses of our people with joy and, therefore, with strength." Listening proudly to the Führer, Porsche was caught short by the announcement that the remarkable vehicle he had designed would henceforth be known as the "Strength-through-Joy Car." "We were horrified," recalled Porsche's son Ferry, who drove Hitler back to the railroad station in a prototype of the little car. "My father commented that we'd never be able to sell the car abroad with such a name." But the designer need not have worried, because no one except obdurate National Socialists ever called it anything but a Volkswagen.

In fact, Ley and his Labor Front colleagues were surprisingly adept at marketing the car. They devised a direct-marketing scheme that was actually a giant layaway plan. A customer paid five marks, or two dollars, a week—about one-sixth of the average worker's take-home pay—and he received a stamp to paste in a savings book in return. After paying installments for fifty-five months, the purchaser would become eligible to receive the Volkswagen—or at least a numbered spot on the waiting list.

All told, precisely 336,668 Germans started buying their people's car on the installment plan, paying some 280 million marks, or 112 million dollars, for savings stamps. But these buyers were destined to be disappointed. On September 1, 1939, before the partially completed plant could deliver a single automobile, Germany invaded Poland, and the Reich was at war.

Hitler ordered Porsche to modify the people's car as an all-purpose

On a gala day at the Volkswagen factory in Wolfsburg in 1938, the Führer climbs aboard a prototype convertible, one of three models that had been designed by Ferdinand Porsche *(shown following Hitler).*

military vehicle. His Volkswagen soon became a soldier's car, plying the roads of Europe, the deserts of North Africa, and the steppes of Russia. At the end of the war, the Russians confiscated the 280 million marks in installment funds from a Berlin bank. But a newly constituted Volkswagen company honored the old savings stamps, and in 1946 the people's car began cruising the autobahn at last. ✚

A Prince of the New Order

From the earliest days of the Nazi movement, Hermann Wilhelm Göring was the most conspicuous member of Adolf Hitler's retinue. Bemedaled and garishly uniformed, his bulky, 280-pound figure became a familiar sight to newsreel viewers throughout the world. The Führer called Göring the "best man I have" and showered him with titles. Reich marshal, commander of the Luftwaffe, president of the Reichstag, Prussian minister of the interior, and controller of the Four-Year Plan, Göring was widely held to be Hitler's heir apparent.

In Hitler's view, Göring was more than a loyal subordinate; he was the "showpiece of the movement." Göring's twenty-two kills as a fighter pilot in the war had earned him a chest full of decorations, including the Pour le mérite, Prussia's highest award for valor. He seemed to personify the virtues of the imperial class that Hitler sought to integrate into his new order.

Göring called himself an "inheritor of all the chivalry of German knighthood." In fact, he was the fourth child of a minor consular official and a Bavarian farm girl. When the family fell on hard times—the senior Göring was aged and ill—they turned to Göring's godfather, Dr. Hermann von Epenstein. A wealthy physician of Jewish ancestry, Epenstein took Frau Göring as his mistress. In return, he allowed the family to live rent-free in the turreted medieval castle of Veldenstein, which Göring later claimed as his family seat.

As the Nazi government's second most powerful official, Göring was able to indulge his aristocratic pretensions to his heart's content. He acquired a slew of luxurious homes and hungrily collected fine art. Inordinately fond of colorful uniforms, Germanic costumes, and fur-trimmed dressing gowns, he often changed outfits three or four times a day.

Foreign observers found the portly clotheshorse more than a little ridiculous; a British diplomat called him the clown of the German revolution. Germans, too, chuckled at the vanity of *der Dicke*, or the Fat One, and Göring jokes were common. But Göring's joviality masked a shrewd, often-ruthless opportunist whose devotion to his Führer never wavered. Hitler, Göring once said, "has been sent us by God to save Germany."

Clad in a ceremonial hunting costume, Hermann Göring assumes a steely-eyed pose that personifies his image as *der Eiserne*—the Iron Man. Appropriately, the central motif of his family crest *(left)* was a mailed fist clutching a silver ring.

In designing Karinhall, Göring indulged a passion for the medieval past. He staged lavish entertainments in the courtyard *(above).*

Lord of Many Manors

As his wealth and power grew, Hermann Göring established a lifestyle few princes could match. His many homes included the Berlin palace of the Reichstag president, a chalet near Hitler's in Berchtesgaden, two castles once owned by his godfather, Dr. Epenstein, an official residence as minister president of Prussia, a Berlin apartment, and a hunting lodge in East Prussia.

But the Reich marshal's favorite residence was a sprawling country house of his own design, erected in the forest of Schorfheide, just forty-five miles north of Berlin. He called it Karinhall, in memory of his Swedish wife Karin, who had died in 1931. In 1934, her remains were brought from Sweden and reinterred in an imposing mausoleum on the grounds of the estate.

Göring arrives at the main entrance to Karinhall in a horse-drawn sleigh *(below)*. He presided over the 100,000-acre estate like a feudal lord.

A nude representing Europa, one of thousands of paintings Göring accumulated, adorns a Karinhall bedroom. Many of the paintings were gifts from industrialists, who were expected to contribute to a Göring art fund.

Although he worried about his weight, Göring enjoyed hosting banquets of game and such traditional favorites as pfefferkuchen in Karinhall's dining room.

Karinhall's library showed Göring's fondness for science fiction, American westerns, and dramas of Shakespeare and Shaw.

An Open House of Treasures

Göring planned every detail of Karinhall, including even the light fixtures and doorknobs—and the result matched his extravagant personality. By 1934, after the place had evolved from a rustic hunting lodge to a veritable treasure house, its walls were covered with the tapestries and paintings of Göring's burgeoning art collection.

The master of Karinhall delighted in conducting grand tours for visiting state dignitaries and celebrities such as Charles and Anne Morrow Lindbergh and the Duke of Windsor. Among the memorable sights on the tour were a candlelit room maintained as a shrine to Karin and a model railway with nearly 2,000 feet of track.

Hermann and Emmy Göring depart Berlin's Lutheran cathedral after their wedding. Hitler is in the group behind them.

An Almost-Royal Wedding

Although he remained devoted to his first wife's memory, Göring remarried four years after Karin's death. His bride was Emmy Sonnemann, a respected actress in the Berlin State Theater. Their wedding on April 10, 1935, became a Nazi extravaganza. Reich Bishop Ludwig Müller presided at the ceremony, and Adolf Hitler served as best man.

The thousands of spectators awaiting a glimpse of the newlyweds prompted a British diplomat to comment, "A visitor to Berlin might well have thought the monarchy had been restored and that he had stumbled upon the preparations for a royal wedding."

SA men and spectators salute the bride and groom as their motorcade passes en route to a reception at Berlin's Opera House.

The Nazi regime's designated partygoer, Göring *(in uniform at upper right)* attends a lavish wedding banquet in Berlin in the spring of 1936.

A corps de ballet performs before Göring, his wife, and guests at the Berlin Opera Ball.

The Great Entertainer

Göring's wealth and aristocratic demeanor, coupled with his convivial personality, made him the ideal host for social luminaries and diplomats from abroad. It proved to be a role that the Führer was glad to have Göring play. Conscious of his own humble origins and ill at ease in social situations, Hitler abhorred such functions. When a conservative Nazi once complained that Göring's extravagance set a bad example in a time of economic austerity, the Führer snapped, "Leave Göring alone! He is the only one who knows how to entertain."

Göring *(at rear)* represents the Reich at a 1936 diplomatic reception in Poland. On the trip, he found time to go hunting for bear.

In a time-honored Junker ritual, Göring accepts the day's trophies on the lawn of his lodge at Rominten Heath in East Prussia.

Master of the Hunt

Despite his girth and love of the good life, Göring was an avid hunter and a crack shot whose happiest hours were spent stalking game in the extensive forests of East Prussia and neighboring Poland. Hitler, who disapproved of hunting, nonetheless indulged his subordinate by appointing him Reich master of the hunt and master of the forest. The title reinforced Göring's image of himself as a Junker of old, and he loved to preside over such traditional hunting ceremonies as the torchlight collection of trophies—animals shot earlier in the day.

Göring, however, was also a pioneer conservationist. He imposed strict regulations on hunting and trapping, drew up laws protecting species that were endangered, initiated an ambitious reforestation program, and created dozens of wildlife preserves.

With a falcon poised on his fist, Reich Master of the Hunt Göring pursues a favorite sport at the game preserve named for him.

Acknowledgments and Picture Credits

The editors thank: England: Braceborough—Diana Moore. London—Clare Blakeway, British Film Institute; Gunn Brinson; Alexandra Weissler, Wiener Institute; Ginny Wood, Imperial War Museum. South Croydon—Brian Leigh Davis. Federal Republic of Germany: Berlin—Heidi Klein, Bildarchiv Preussischer Kulturbesitz; Gabrielle Kohler-Gallei, Archiv für Kunst und Geschichte; Wolfgang Streubel, Ullstein Bilderdienst. Bonn—Holger Feldmann-Marth, Archiv, Sozialdemokratische Partei Deutschlands. Göttingen—Christian Graf von Krockow. Hamburg—Heinz Höhne; Jochen von Lang. Koblenz—Meinrad Nilges, Bundesarchiv. Hanover—Herbert Döler; Egon Kuhn, Freizeitheim. Northeim—Hartmut von Hindte, Stadtarchiv. Munich—Elisabeth Heidt, Süddeutscher Verlag Bilderdienst; Robert Hoffmann; Peter Wagner, Hermann Historica. Stuttgart—Sabine Oppenländer, Bibliothek für Zeitgeschichte. France: Paris—Christophe Thomas, Direction des Status et de l'Information, Ministère des Anciens Combattants. German Democratic Republic: Berlin—Hannes Quaschinsky, ADN-Zentralbild. Plauen—Walter and Henni Ballhause. United States: District of Columbia—Dr. Steve Goodell, Susan Moganstein, Holocaust Memorial Museum; Margaret Shannon, Library of Congress. Michigan: Detroit—Prof. Guy Stern. Virginia: Springfield—George Petersen.

Credits from left to right are separated by semicolons, from top to bottom by dashes. Cover: AP/Wide World Photos. 4, 5: Walter Ballhause, Plauen, GDR. 6: Stadt Northeim, Stadtarchiv. 8, 9: R. R. Donnelley Cartographic Services. 10, 11: J. H. Darchinger, Bonn. 12: Trustees of The Imperial War Museum, London. 13: Bundesarchiv, Koblenz. 15-18: Walter Ballhause, Plauen, GDR. 20, 21: Larry Sherer, courtesy Stephen L. Flood. 23: Archiv der Sozialen Demokratie, Bonn. 24: Walter Ballhause, Plauen, GDR. 25: Larry Sherer, courtesy Stephen L. Flood. 29: Larry Sherer, courtesy William A. Xanten (3)—Thomas Wittmann—William A. Xanten (2)—Thomas Wittmann. 30: Bundesarchiv, Koblenz. 31: Keystone Press, New York. 32, 33: Ullstein Bilderdienst, West Berlin. 35: Bundesarchiv, Koblenz. 36, 37: Bundesarchiv, Koblenz, except top right KZ-Gedenkstätte, Dachau. 39: Bundesarchiv, Koblenz. 42, 43: Stadt Northeim, Stadtarchiv. 44, 45: National Archives, no. 131-GR-164-29, inset Süddeutscher Verlag Bilderdienst, Munich. 46, 47: Bildarchiv Preussischer Kulturbesitz (BPK), West Berlin, inset Mike and Mark Chenault, Albert Speer Archive, Dallas. 48, 49: BPK, West Berlin, inset Süddeutscher Verlag Bilderdienst, Munich. 50, 51: Stadt Nürnberg, Hochbauamt, inset BPK, West Berlin. 52: Larry Sherer, from *Der Zweite Weltkrieg* by Raymond Cartier, R. Piper, Munich, 1967. 54: Presseillustrationen Heinrich R. Hoffmann, Munich. 55: Ullstein Bilderdienst, West Berlin. 56: BPK, West Berlin. 57: Bundesarchiv, Koblenz, except second from right BPK, West Berlin. 58, 59: Landeskirchliches Archiv, Nuremberg—Stadtbibliothek Nürnberg, foto Hilbinger. 61: National Archives, no. 242-HB-18156a1a. 62: Süddeutscher Verlag Bilderdienst, Munich. 63: Hugo Jaeger, LIFE Magazine, © Time Inc. 65: Weidenfeld (Publishers) Ltd., London. 66, 67: Presseillustrationen Heinrich R. Hoffmann, Munich—Bundesarchiv, Koblenz. 68: The Weimar Archive, Telford. 70: Ullstein Bilderdienst, West Berlin. 71: National Film Archive, London. 72, 73: Library of Congress. 74: Keystone Pressedienst, Hamburg; National Archives, no. 242-HB-17954. 75: Bundesarchiv, Koblenz. 76: Library of Congress—Larry Sherer, from *Legion Condor, 1936-1939,* by Karl Ries and Hans Ring, Dieter Hoffmann, Mainz, 1980. 79-82: All photos from Nazi Book Burnings and the American Response, an exhibition by the Library of Congress and the United States Holocaust Memorial Museum, Washington, D.C. 79: ADN-Zentralbild, Berlin, GDR, courtesy Professor Guy Stern Collection. 80, 81: National Archives, from the film *The Nazi Plan, 1945,* except lower left A. Pisarek/BPK, West Berlin. 83: UPI/Bettmann Newsphotos. 84, 85: Hugo Jaeger, LIFE Magazine, © Time Inc. 86: SPD Friedrich-Ebert-Stiftung, Bonn Foto Werner Schüring. 87: Weidenfeld (Publishers) Ltd., London. 88: David French, courtesy Roger S. Steffen Historical Militaria. 89: Lothar Rübelt/Black Star. 90, 91: Library of Congress, from *XI. Olympiade Berlin, 1936: Amtlicher Bericht,* Wilhelm Limpert, Berlin SW 68, 1937; Ullstein Bilderdienst, West Berlin. 92: Edimedia, Paris. 93: Ullstein Bilderdienst, West Berlin. 94, 95: Library of Congress, from *Champions in Action* by Frank A. Wrensch, photos by Dr. Paul Wolff, William Morrow, New York, 1938; Süddeutscher Verlag Bilderdienst, Munich—Library of Congress, from *XI. Olympiade Berlin, 1936: Amtlicher Bericht,* Wilhelm Limpert, Berlin SW 68, 1937. 96: Ullstein Bilderdienst, West Berlin. 97: BPK, West Berlin. 98: Bundesarchiv, Koblenz. 100: Walter Ballhause, Plauen, GDR. 103: Stadtarchiv, Nuremberg. 104, 105: Larry Sherer, courtesy Stephen L. Flood. 107: Süddeutscher Verlag Bilderdienst, Munich. 108, 109: Bundesarchiv, Koblenz; Popperfoto, London. 110, 111: Background photo Archives Tallandier, Paris. Insets, Larry Sherer, courtesy Alfred Presti; Michael E. Crimens; Gary Gerber; Michael E. Crimens—Alfred Presti (3). 113: Department of Rare Books, William R. Perkins Library, Duke University. 117: AP/Wide World Photos. 119: BPK, West Berlin. 120, 121: Larry Sherer, from *"Deutsche Frauen und Mädchen!"* by Norbert Westenrieder, Droste, Düsseldorf, 1984, except top right Larry Sherer, courtesy George A. Petersen. 122: Süddeutscher Verlag Bilderdienst, Munich. 123: Larry Sherer, courtesy George A. Petersen. 124: Süddeutscher Verlag Bilderdienst, Munich. 125: Landesbildstelle, Berlin. 126, 127: Süddeutscher Verlag Bilderdienst, Munich. 128, 129: BPK, West Berlin; Larry Sherer, from *Hitler* by John Toland, Doubleday, Garden City, N.Y., 1978. 130: Ullstein Bilderdienst, West Berlin. 132, 133: Freelance Photographers Guild. 134, 135: Bundesarchiv, Koblenz, inset BPK, West Berlin. 136, 137: The Keystone Collection, London, inset Bundesarchiv, Koblenz. 138, 139: Ullstein Bilderdienst, West Berlin. 140, 141: Süddeutscher Verlag Bilderdienst, Munich. 142, 143: UPI/Bettmann Newsphotos. 144: Stadtarchiv, Frankfurt. 146: Bibliothèque Nationale, Paris—National Archives, no. 242-HB-4980. 149: BPK, West Berlin. 151: Bundesarchiv, Koblenz. 152: BPK, West Berlin. 153: Ullstein Bilderdienst, West Berlin. 154: Larry Sherer, courtesy George A. Petersen. 156: Süddeutscher Verlag Bilderdienst, Munich. 157: Freelance Photographers Guild. 158: Süddeutscher Verlag Bilderdienst, Munich. 162: Bundesarchiv, Koblenz. 163: Ullstein Bilderdienst, West Berlin. 164, 165: Süddeutscher Verlag Bilderdienst, Munich. 167: BPK, West Berlin. 168: Archiv für Kunst und Geschichte, West Berlin; BPK, West Berlin—badges, Larry Sherer, courtesy Alfred Presti. 169: Bundesarchiv, Koblenz (2)—badges, Larry Sherer, courtesy Ron Wolin; Thom Furgason; George A. Petersen; Joan Panettière. 171: Süddeutscher Verlag Bilderdienst, Munich—Otto Spronk. 172, 173: Süddeutscher Verlag Bilderdienst, Munich. 174: Hermann Historica, Munich, foto Patzelt, courtesy Tom Johnson. 175: D. V. from Black Star. 176, 177: BPK, West Berlin; Ernst Sandau, Berlin. 178, 179: BPK, West Berlin; Ernst Sandau, Berlin (2). 180, 181: Library of Congress. 182, 183: Library of Congress, except lower left Larry Sherer, from *XI. Olympiade Berlin, 1936: Amtlicher Bericht,* Wilhelm Limpert, Berlin SW 68, 1937. 184, 185: Archiv für Kunst und Geschichte, West Berlin; Library of Congress.

Bibliography

Allen, William Sheridan, *The Nazi Seizure of Power: The Experience of a Single German Town, 1922-1945*. New York: Franklin Watts, 1984.

Bewley, Charles, *Hermann Göring and the Third Reich*. Toronto: Devin-Adair, 1962.

Boberach, Heinz, *Jugend unter Hitler*. Düsseldorf: Droste, 1982.

Boelcke, Willi A., ed., *The Secret Conferences of Dr Goebbels, October 1939-March 1943*. Transl. by Ewald Osers. London: Weidenfeld and Nicolson, 1967.

Bracher, Karl Dietrich, *The German Dictatorship*. Transl. by Jean Steinberg. New York: Praeger, 1970.

Broszat, Martin, *Hitler and the Collapse of Weimar Germany*. Transl. by V. R. Berghahn. Leamington Spa, England: Berg, 1987.

Burden, Hamilton T., *The Nuremberg Party Rallies, 1923-39*. New York: Praeger, 1967.

Chenault, Mike, and Mark Chenault, *The New Germany, 1933-1945*. Dallas: Taylor, 1987.

Conway, J. S., *The Nazi Persecution of the Churches, 1933-45*. New York: Basic Books, 1968.

Dietrich, Otto, *Hitler*. Transl. by Richard Winston and Clara Winston. Chicago: Henry Regnery, 1955.

Eckert, Georg, ed., *1863-1963: Hundert Jahre Deutsche Sozialdemokratie*. Hanover: J. H. W. Dietz Nachf., 1963.

Engelmann, Bernt, *In Hitler's Germany*. Transl. by Krishna Winston. New York: Pantheon Books, 1986.

Farquharson, J. E., *The Plough and the Swastika*. London: Sage, 1976.

Frei, Bruno, ed., *The Stolen Republic: Selected Writings of Carl von Ossietzky*. London: Lawrence and Wishart, 1971.

Frischauer, Willi, *The Rise and Fall of Hermann Goering*. Boston: Houghton Mifflin, 1951.

Fritzsch, Robert, *Nürnberg unterm Hakenkreuz*. Düsseldorf: Droste, 1983.

Grunberger, Richard, *The 12-Year Reich*. New York: Holt, Rinehart and Winston, 1971.

Grunfeld, Frederic V., *The Hitler File*. New York: Random House, 1974.

Hale, Oron J., *The Captive Press in the Third Reich*. Princeton, N.J.: Princeton Univ. Press, 1964.

Handrick, Gotthardt, "Als Deutscher Jagdflieger in Spanien." *Die Wehrmacht* (Berlin), June 7, 1939.

Hecht, Ingeborg, *Invisible Walls: A German Family under the Nuremberg Laws*. Transl. by J. Maxwell Brownjohn. San Diego: Harcourt Brace Jovanovich, 1985.

Heiber, Helmut, *Goebbels*. Transl. by John K. Dickinson. New York: Hawthorn Books, 1972.

Helmreich, Ernst Christian, *The German Churches under Hitler*. Detroit: Wayne State Univ. Press, 1979.

Holmes, Judith, *Olympiad 1936*. New York: Ballantine Books, 1971.

Hopfinger, K. B., *The Volkswagen Story*. Cambridge, Mass.: Robert Bentley, 1971.

Hull, David Stewart, *Film in the Third Reich*. Berkeley: Univ. of California Press, 1969.

Kater, Michael H., *The Nazi Party*. Cambridge, Mass.: Harvard Univ. Press, 1983.

Kempowski, Walter, ed. *Did You Ever See Hitler?* Transl. by Michael Roloff. New York: Avon Books, 1975.

Kershaw, Ian, *Popular Opinion and Political Dissent in the Third Reich: Bavaria, 1933-1945*. Oxford: Clarendon, 1983.

Kiersch, Gerhard, et al., *Berliner Alltag im Dritten Reich*. Düsseldorf: Droste, 1981.

Koch, H. W.:
Hitler Youth. New York: Ballantine Books, 1972.
The Hitler Youth: Origins and Development, 1922-45. New York: Dorset, 1988.

Koehn, Ilse, *Mischling, Second Degree*. New York: Greenwillow Books, 1977.

Koonz, Claudia, *Mothers in the Fatherland*. New York: St. Martin's, 1987.

Krüger, Horst, *A Crack in the Wall: Growing Up under Hitler*. Transl. by Ruth Hein. New York: Fromm International, 1982.

Kusch, Eugen, *Nürnberg*. Nuremberg: Nürnberger Presse, 1958.

Laqueur, Walter Z., *Young Germany: A History of the German Youth Movement*. New York: Basic Books, 1962.

Lewy, Guenter, *The Catholic Church and Nazi Germany*. New York: McGraw-Hill, 1964.

Littlejohn, David, *The Hitler Youth*. Somerset, Ky.: Agincourt, 1988.

Mandell, Richard D., *The Nazi Olympics*. Urbana: Univ. of Illinois Press, 1987.

Manvell, Roger, *Göring*. New York: Ballantine Books, 1972.

Manvell, Roger, and Heinrich Fraenkel, *The German Cinema*. New York: Praeger, 1971.

Maschmann, Melita, *Account Rendered*. Transl. by Geoffrey Strachan. London: Abelard-Schuman, 1964.

Mommsen, Hans, Karl Otmar, and Ulrich Cartarius, eds., *The German Resistance Movement, 1933-1945*. Stuttgart: Institut für Auslandsbeziehungen, 1983.

Mosley, Leonard, *The Reich Marshal*. Garden City, N.Y.: Doubleday, 1974.

Nelson, Walter Henry, *Small Wonder: The Amazing Story of the Volkswagen*. Boston: Little, Brown, 1970.

Noakes, Jeremy, ed., *Government, Party and People in Nazi Germany*. Exeter, England: Univ. of Exeter, 1980.

Noakes, J., and G. Pridham, eds., *State, Economy, and Society, 1933-39*. Vol. 2 of *Nazism, 1919-1945*. Exeter, England: Univ. of Exeter, 1984.

Orlow, Dietrich, *The History of the Nazi Party, 1933-1945*. Pittsburgh: Univ. of Pittsburgh Press, 1973.

Peterson, Edward N., *The Limits of Hitler's Power*. Princeton, N.J.: Princeton Univ. Press, 1969.

Peukert, Detlev J. K., *Inside Nazi Germany*. Transl. by Richard Deveson. New Haven, Conn.: Yale Univ. Press, 1987.

Remak, Joachim, ed., *The Nazi Years*. New York: Simon and Schuster, 1969.

Richardson, Horst Fuchs, ed. and transl., *Sieg Heil! War Letters of Tank Gunner Karl Fuchs, 1937-1941*. Hamden, Conn.: Archon Books, 1987.

Rubenstein, Richard L., and John K. Roth, *Approaches to Auschwitz*. Atlanta: John Knox, 1987.

Ruppert, Wolfgang, *Fotogeschichte der Deutschen Sozialdemokratie*. Ed. by Willy Brandt. Berlin: Siedler, 1988.

Rutherford, Ward, *Hitler's Propaganda Machine*. London: Bison Books, 1978.

Schoenbaum, David, *Hitler's Social Revolution*. Garden City, N.Y.: Doubleday, 1966.

Snyder, Louis L., *Encyclopedia of the Third Reich*. New York: McGraw-Hill, 1976.

Speer, Albert, *Inside the Third Reich*. Transl. by Richard Winston and Clara Winston. New York: Macmillan, 1970.

Stachura, Peter D., ed., *The Shaping of the Nazi State*. London: Croom Helm, 1978.

Stephenson, Jill, *Women in Nazi Society*. New York: Barnes & Noble, 1975.

Toland, John, *Hitler*. Garden City, N.Y.: Doubleday, 1978.

Turner, Henry Ashby, Jr., ed., *Hitler*. Transl. by Ruth Hein. New Haven, Conn.: Yale Univ. Press, 1985.

Walther, Herbert, ed., *Hitler*. New York: Exeter Books, 1984.

Westenrieder, Norbert, *"Deutsche Frauen und Mädchen!"* Düsseldorf: Droste, 1984.

Wistrich, Robert, *Who's Who in Nazi Germany*. New York: Bonanza Books, 1984.

Wunder, Thomas, *Das Reichsparteitagsgelände in Nürnberg*. Nuremberg: Kunstpädagogisches Zentrum im Germanischen Nationalmuseum, 1984.

Zassenhaus, Hiltgunt, *Walls: Resisting the Third Reich—One Woman's Story*. Boston: Beacon, 1974.

Index

Numerals in italics indicate an illustration of the subject mentioned.

M011550290